NAMATH

by Rose Namath Szolnoki
with Bill Kushner

MY SON JOE

Library of Congress Catalog Card Number: 75-12417

Manufactured in the United States of America

First Printing 1975

Namath My Son Joe

Editor: Karen Phillips

Dedication

To my five children, Rita, Sonny, Bobby,
Franklin, and Joe; to my eighteen grandchildren
and one great grandchild; to Jimmy Walsh, Joe's
attorney; and to all the Joe Namath fans
everywhere.

I would like to thank these people who went the
"extra mile" in helping with this book: Art
Catrino, Jack Warner, Dr. and Mrs. Maxwell
Moody, Dr. and Mrs. James Kightlinger, and Mr.
Jack Merle.

Always a Rose
by
Joe Namath

Namath, My Son Joe is the true story of my life, exactly the way my mother thought it happened. Seriously though, when you think about it, my mother probably knows more about me than I know about myself. After all, she was there the day my story started and has been part of my life ever since. The only problem is that my mother has a knack for getting everything sort of twisted up, and then before you know it, she has everyone else mixed up. It would be like Mom marching in a parade to the sound of a different drummer and then convincing everyone else they were out of step. That's the way Mom is.

Like when the Jets were going to play the Colts in the Super Bowl of 1969. We were seventeen point underdogs and I was getting worried. I called home to gently break the news of the spot on the game to Mom. I didn't want her to think the Colts were going to run roughshod, so I said with a laugh, "Mom, did you hear the spot on the game is seventeen points?"

"Joey, honey!" she exclaimed excitedly. "Do you think you can win by that many points?"

My mother is great with words and before she was finished, I thought the Colts were twenty-four point underdogs. In fact, I was disappointed when we only beat them 16–7. Mom was too.

She sighed after the game, "Gee, Joey, if you would have only thrown another touchdown pass or two, you could have really beaten them good."

"But, Mom," I explained, "I didn't even throw one touchdown pass."

"Well, dear, I'm sure that if you wanted to, you could have."

Of course, she was right.

I remember once when she came up to New York for a visit. I was busy with practice, and she was getting lonely sitting around the apartment all day. We made arrangements for her sister-in-law (my Aunt Anna) to fly in from Beaver Falls. Mom and Aunt Anna are traveling buddies, and they would have a great time.

Since I was busy, a friend of mine Al Hassan volunteered to pick up Aunt Anna at the airport and Mom went along "just for the ride." People were rushing all over the place at Kennedy Airport, so Al instructed Mom to sit tight while he searched out Aunt Anna. It took Mom about thirty seconds of sitting tight to figure out Aunt Anna was on the other side of the airport. A normal person would just walk around to the other side through the terminal building, find Aunt Anna, and come back into the city. But not my Mom. Before it was over the police were on the scene, hundreds of people were watching, and Al was nearly on his way to jail.

It started when Mom, reasoning that the shortest distance between two points is a straight line, decided to just cross the runway to the other side. A police officer happened to spy a lady running across the runway ducking and dodging planes and put the old pinch on her when she arrived. In his pleasant New Yorker manner of speaking, the officer wanted to know exactly what Mom was doing out on the runway.

"Why officer, I was just coming over here from over there."

The officer patiently explained that she could have been seriously injured.

"Oh no, officer. I was very careful. I would never let that happen. Even when I cross the street I look. . . ." Of course the explanation was cut short by the officer asking more questions and giving more vivid examples of what might have happened to her. By now, people were milling around looking strangely at Mom, and when she tried to explain about Aunt Anna and that she was Joe Namath's mother, well, I don't have to tell you what everyone thought.

Al finally came to the rescue, and before long Mom started to say it was Al's fault. "After all, he told me to wait over there. He wouldn't listen when I told him we were on the wrong side of the airport. Why, Aunt Anna could have been lost!" Mom was real convincing, and now the officer wanted to know why Al left my mother over there all alone.

Then Aunt Anna came to Al's rescue, and before long everything was settled and back to normal. In all, it was just an average day in the life of my mother.

Now, don't get the idea this book is going to be that confusing. Really it's not. Most of it will be real smooth and easy to understand. Like when Mom came to visit me in Alabama. My brother Franklin put her on the plane at Pittsburgh with a warning about Atlanta. "Mom," Franklin said, "the plane lands in Atlanta . . . don't get off. It will only be there a few minutes and then it will fly nonstop into Tuscaloosa. Then Joey will pick you up."

You guessed it. Mom got off in Atlanta. But it wasn't her fault. Franklin mentioned something about "nonstop" and the captain of the plane mumbled something about "Tuscaloosa," so Mom got off in Atlanta.

Or there's the time my mother called me and she was crying. I couldn't understand her over the phone and was getting scared. "Mom, slow down. What's the matter?"

Then I got it out of her. "Sammy ate my teeth!"

Poor Sammy. He was our dog, and the dummy ate my mother's teeth. She had just gotten a new set of false teeth and they hurt her gums. She took them out, laid them on the coffee table, and went into the kitchen. The dumb dog just chewed them to bits and pieces. But Mom said, "That crazy dog should have known better."

Mom explained this to Sammy and even to this day, the dog puts his tail between his legs and hides under the couch when someone mentions teeth.

Well, I think you can see what I mean about my mother. She is really different. In fact, people always say, "Joe, your mother is really different." I could go on and tell you a lot about her, but most of the story is right here in this book. Of course, it is my mother's version of my quiet life . . . my uneventful life.

I love my mother, and doesn't everyone love his mother? If I could pick anyone in the world to be my mother, I'd pick the same one that God gave me when I came into this world. For I know all mothers are beautiful flowers, and I know He gave me a Rose.

NAMATH MY SON JOE

In the rugged hill country of western Pennsylvania, not quite fifty miles northwest of Pittsburgh, lies the sleepy little community of Beaver Falls, population 14,500. I don't know how they came to name this place. I guess at one time there might have been a lot of beavers out there in the woods and maybe even a waterfall or two on the Beaver River that runs through town. But if there ever were, it was long before the steel mills came to town, because during my lifetime I've never seen a beaver, and the river hardly makes a ripple now, much less a waterfall.

I suppose to an outsider, or maybe even to some people like myself who have lived here all of their lives, Beaver Falls isn't a garden spot. It's hardly a vacation resort or a Shangri-La. It's special to me; I love the people here and I wouldn't live anywhere else. But, in all honesty, what Beaver Falls is, is a steel mill town. It's one of many that lie by the river in the Beaver Valley along with cities like Aliquippa, Sharon, Ambridge, Farrell, and New Castle, cities that in this century, at least, seem to have produced two things—a lot of steel and a lot of football players, including one you're getting ready to learn a few things about that maybe you didn't know before: my son the quarterback—Joe Namath.

4   All of the cities in the valley, part of the great steel-producing region of America that stretches from Pittsburgh in the southwest to Youngstown, Ohio, in the northwest, seem to look alike. In fact, if it weren't for the signs along the way, you might have a hard time telling where you were. The mills belong to some pretty famous companies, such as Republic Steel, Moltrup Steel, Armstrong Cork Company, and Babcock and Wilcox, and for years they have been the lifeblood of the entire valley. The mills came here for two reasons: The Beaver Valley was close to the great coal-producing region of the northeast, and the valley offered easy transportation, originally by the Beaver River, which flows south of here for a few miles until it joins the mighty Ohio, and later by the railroad tracks that were handily laid along the riverbed.

The start of Beaver Falls itself is Geneva College, which sits up on College Hill at the north end of town. From the top of the hill you can see the red haze from the mills that even today settles over the town. From there, you can take Route 18 and head south to where it bends left and then right and becomes Seventh Avenue—the main drag right through the center of town. Along the way are rows and rows of two-story wooden frame houses jammed so close together that sometimes you have a hard time seeing between them. At one time, I suspect, all of these houses were painted white, but they quickly lost their color under a constant barrage of dirt and grime from the mills. I remember from my childhood and even later that every time the Sears Roebuck store would have a sale on dark green paint all of a sudden three or four houses in a row would change their color almost overnight. Under the circumstances, dark green proved to be a more practical color.

Downtown Beaver Falls begins at Nineteenth Street. Here the buildings are small—nothing bigger than three stories—and they house businesses like the shoe store, the Farmers Bank, and the Beaver Falls *News-Tribune,* our very own daily newspaper. Even though Beaver Falls is my hometown, I've got to admit we sure have made a mess of the parking situation. We apparently haven't discovered parallel parking yet, and all the cars have to park perpendicular to the sidewalks. You can always tell a car from Beaver Falls because its right side is bound to be scraped from its front fender all the way to the back from brushing into the rear ends of those big, modern automobiles that stick out halfway across the street.

There are attractive areas in town. One is called Ross Hill, which is actually outside of Beaver Falls in a community called Patterson Heights, and another is a five-block stretch along Seventh Avenue between Seventeenth Street and Twelfth Street. In these sections of town the houses are made of brick, not wood, and there's a little more room between them. Also, each one has a neat, little hedge around the small front yard, and that little hedge is the status symbol of Beaver Falls.

If you continue on down Seventh Avenue from the business district, you drive down a little bit of a hill and across the railroad tracks and all of a sudden you're in the lower end of town—literally the "other side of the tracks." This is where I lived most of my life. But even though I called it home, in all honesty, it wasn't a very pretty place. There was the Economy Supermarket where I did most of my shopping, a pool hall, a beer garden, a flea market, a shoe repair shop, and a lot of windows that I'll bet hadn't been washed in fifty years. Today, a lot of those windows are boarded up. In this part of town the frame houses—or maybe an occasional brick house—sit side by side, interrupted only by the barbed wire that surrounds the junkyards and factories in the neighborhood.

There are two buildings of special interest, especially the way things have turned out over the last twenty years or so. At the corner of Seventeenth Street and Seventh Avenue there is a large two-story structure that's simply called Middle School. You probably think of it as a junior high school, but it was really just the ninth grade, where the kids of Beaver Falls went for one year before they moved on to high school. The Middle School is a monument to the sand and gravel industry. There are no trees, no flowers, and no grass around anywhere; the school is entirely surrounded by that good old maintenance-free cement. Kids who grew up on the playgrounds of the big eastern cities will know what I'm talking about.

One block behind the Middle School, on Eighth Avenue, is Beaver Falls High School, which from the outside certainly looks like an institution. It's made entirely of orange brick. Behind the high school is a huge athletic field that makes the Middle School playground look beautiful. The high school field is just dirt—no grass and only a few burned-out weeds—and it is surrounded by broken bleachers and ripped down, rusty fences. The hillside beyond is hardly any prettier. Streams of raw sewage trickle down between an assortment of junk and garbage that includes everything from broken bottles to tin cans to newspapers to old toilet seats. And that is where my son Joey learned how to play football.

When Bill Kushner, the gentleman who is helping me with this book, first saw the high school field, he said it held him in complete awe. He said it was miserable and wretched. That was quite a remark considering Bill comes from another valley community called Sharon, where the football field can't be too much nicer.

Maybe our field is primitive, but it is this kind of an environment that has produced some of the finest college and professional football players in America, and I'm not just talking about Joe Namath. Every year there is probably a richer harvest from the cities of the Beaver Valley than from any other place its size in America. Babe Parelli, who was a pretty fair quarterback under Bear Bryant at the University of Kentucky, is from Rochester. Mike Ditka, who a lot of people say may have been the finest tight end ever, is from Aliquippa. Then just down the river a little from the town of Ambridge, came a fellow by the name of Mike Lucci. He plays linebacker for the Detroit Lions, and I've more to say about him later. Terry Hanratty, the all-American from Notre Dame who is now with the world champion Pittsburgh Steelers, is from Butler, and Jim Mutscheller and Joe Walton, both of them all-pro ends, are from right here in Beaver Falls.

There's a reason for this, of course. It doesn't take a Beaver Falls father—or any other father in the valley—much time in the hot mill of one of those steel companies to know he doesn't want his own sons working there if he can possibly help it. But Beaver Falls isn't the kind of place where you can just up and leave. You've got to earn your way out somehow, and for the boys the best way has always been through college, through an athletic scholarship. Bear Bryant, who is now coaching down there at the University of Alabama, has always said that poor boys are easier to coach and tend to play harder than rich boys—because they're trying to escape.

Now as for me, I don't ever want to leave Beaver Falls. I've had the chance in recent years, and there were plenty of times earlier in my life when I might have wished to get out and couldn't, but right now all of my friends are here in the valley, and I just don't know where I could be happier if I left.

Since I'm already starting to talk about football a little bit, I should say something right here and now. I've been a Joe Namath fan my whole life, being his mother and all. When he was in high school, I saw just about every home game Joe played. When he was at Alabama, I watched that Crimson Tide roll whenever it was on television or kept that radio going every Saturday until I got the score of the game; I even saw a few in person. And now that he's a big celebrity with the pros I watch him on television every Sunday. But I still don't know a whole lot of details about football. So every time you run across some football talk in this book, things like audibles, slants, 4–3 defenses, and whatever other crazy names they have for things, you can be pretty sure my collaborator, Bill Kushner, had a hand in it. Bill was a fine collegiate quarterback himself, and he's been a friend of Joe's and mine ever since 1970 when he spent eight weeks in the New York Jets' camp. So he knows a whole lot more football than I do, and you can be pretty sure that anytime I talk about things that happened right down there on the field, it comes mainly from Bill. All the rest of this book comes from me, Joe's mother.

I was born right here in Beaver Falls on April 21, 1912, under the sign of Taurus, which gives you a clue to my age and maybe even to my personality, and right away I was baptized Rosal Juhasz—that's pronounced *You*-house—by two fine Hungarian parents, Alexander and Rose Juhasz. Both of my parents were immigrants who had been brought over from the old country by my mother's father. What happened was this: Grandfather Paul Simon came over first and found a place for his family and his in-laws to live; then he sent over for the rest of his relatives to join him. My mother remembered the trip vividly right up until the day she died. She and the others were jammed in steerage class of a very slow boat that took thirty-one days to cross the Atlantic, and it was impossible for her to believe that in her lifetime she could have made the same trip in six hours.

My parents came to America just about the time the steel mills were springing up all along the Beaver Valley and attracting the strong men of Central Europe—Poles, Czechs, and Hungarians—who were willing to exchange a long day's work in the heat and dirt of the mills for a paycheck and the promise of the American dream. Sometimes the paychecks weren't very big, but they provided for a life that was better than any the immigrants could possibly have known in the old country.

Life was always hard, though. I was just one of two brothers and two sisters of devout Catholic parents—big families were more common in those days—and there weren't a lot of luxuries. Everyone was expected to pitch in and help with the work load just as soon as he or she could. I was a big baby—my parents said I tipped the scales at more than twelve pounds when I was born—and it didn't seem like too many years later before I was doing the wash, cleaning the house, and even stoking the furnace.

I went to St. Mary's High School, but my education stopped when I graduated from the twelfth grade, which was not uncommon then. Women in mill towns were expected to work just as soon as they could, then find a husband when they came of age and settle down to raise families of their own.

I would like to quickly add, however, that my son Joe isn't the only athlete in his family, nor the only rebel. Not by a long shot. When I was in the eighth grade at St. Mary's, I played on the girls' basketball team—until I showed up for a game one day wearing black shorts instead of regulation bloomers. Talk about shocking people! The poor sisters at the school couldn't take that at all, and my athletic career was nipped in the bud.

When I turned nineteen, in 1931, I decided to get married. John Namath was my handsome beau and my parents were delighted. He was a nice young fellow whose parents, like mine, had immigrated to Beaver Falls from a little town in Hungary, and in everybody's eyes it was a perfect match. He had a good job at the Moltrup Steel Company as a helper on a hot furnace, and he was a big, good-looking, hard-working man. But from my point of view, I was honestly less concerned about getting married than I was with the fact that at last I was finished with all that hard work around the Juhasz household.

At least that was my thought at the time. But things didn't exactly work out that way because it didn't seem we had been married two weeks when something called the Depression hit Beaver Falls. My marriage was the start of a six-year period in my life I'll never forget. Never.

Almost all the mills in Beaver Falls and in the other valley communities closed down—all except Moltrup Steel. They never laid a man off, even if they could only give a man a half-day's work every two weeks. The Depression hit so fast that by the time we got married John was already working just two days a week. Then it got worse. I remember one day when he brought the pay home, and after the mill had deducted everything, his check was for exactly ten cents. I would have framed it except we needed that dime so badly. The thing that kept us going was that John worked part time at Sedicoff's Shoe Store, where he made a nickel after every dollar. That is, if he sold a pair of shoes for $2.98, he got to keep fifteen cents. It doesn't sound like much, but to us it was big money. I got a part-time job as a saleslady at Montgomery Ward for a while, and another time I got a job working as a maid, I guess you'd call it, for a nice doctor up in Patterson Heights, that real swank community right next to Beaver Falls. Working in Patterson Heights turned out to be pretty ironic for me because I live there now myself, but in those days the idea of living in a house up on Ross Hill was just about the farthest thing in the world from my mind. I worked on Saturdays from eight o'clock in the morning until five o'clock at night for one dollar, and I did it because that dollar bought a lot of groceries. When you shopped downtown, you could get five pounds of hamburger for a quarter and six nice pork chops for another quarter, but it wasn't very often you had the money to buy meat. That was a real luxury. It's funny, but today some people will walk right past a penny if they see one on the sidewalk; if you were in Beaver Falls in the 1930s, you broke your back to pick one up.

Somehow, though, we all managed to eat pretty well. Nobody was thin because we ate a lot of fattening foods. It probably wasn't the best-balanced diet in the world but at least we all looked healthy. One week I'd serve tomato soup, then potato soup, and then some other kind of homemade soup and maybe some rice. The next week I'd serve tomato soup again and start all over. Everybody planted their own gardens, when they could, and baked their own bread, and I made my own apple butter, which was very good, to put on the bread. We raised rabbits for food, too, and we ate a lot of them; so many, in fact, you couldn't feed me a piece of rabbit today if that's all you had to offer.

John and his brothers and my brothers would go fishing sometimes and go up into the hills to pick apples and blackberries. One time they even brought home the wrong kind of mushrooms and everybody got sick but me and our dog, Princie. We wouldn't touch them; Princie took one smell and left the room.

Princie, who was a good old mongrel, helped out with the family economy, too. He and the other neighborhood dogs hung around the wholesale meat factory in Beaver Falls and waited for the butchers to throw out meat scraps and fat. Well, Princie ate the meat but brought home the fat, which I boiled and strained down into something called leaf lard—and that's what I made our soap out of.

No, there just weren't many luxuries. There was no such thing as coffee anytime you wanted it or lard, except what Princie brought home, or soap powder. It just wasn't available. For example, if somebody in the neighborhood found out one of the stores was having a sale on soap powder, all of us wives ran down there immediately, even with our aprons on sloppy wet, to get some.

Clothes were hard to come by, too. My mother made pillow covers, sheets, petticoats, and even underpants out of flour sacks. And you could tell who the woman was coming up the street long before you really got a good look at her, because everybody owned just one dress—sometimes two if she was lucky—and you got to recognize everybody by that one dress. I, myself, wore one dress for six years, a big, polka-dotted thing I came to hate. That wasn't just my good dress, it was my only dress.

Nobody could afford to go anywhere, of course. John and I sure didn't own a car. But it's strange, because there was real harmony among the families in the neighborhood during those hard times. Everybody stayed at home and listened to the radio—my favorite program was "Amos 'n Andy"—or played cards or just sat around and popped popcorn while we talked. I guess it was kind of forced upon us, but there was a real sense of participation in the neighborhood. For example, four or five entire families used to get together at our house during the evening so they could shut off their electricity and save money. Then the next time we'd go over to somebody else's house so we could turn off ours. Those were hard times and I never want to go through them again, but what I remember most is that not too many people were bitter, really bitter. Most people were happy, or at least made do with what they had, and it was a real

time of sharing. But at the same time—and this may be pretty
obvious—those Depression years did a whole lot to shape our later lives and attitudes, and more importantly, they shaped the attitudes and values of the kids who were born then.

When we were first married, John and I decided we would put off having kids for a while because of our finances, but I quickly felt trapped. John had his work, when it was available, but in that first year of marriage I didn't feel I had anything constructive to do except the work around the house, which is what I'd gotten married to avoid in the first place. To fill that void in my life, we did decide to start our family.

And so in late 1932, just before Christmas, our home was blessed with the arrival of a baby boy, John Alexander Namath. His proud father would not consider any other name.

Three, I felt, was a nice number for a family. John—or Sonny, as we quickly came to call him—was a joy to me, and he certainly did fill that void. And how. I don't know whether Sonny got his character traits from the Namath or the Juhasz side of the family, probably a little bit of both. But he was a rambunctious little thing and not too much later a rambunctious big thing. I really loved the feisty fellow, though, for all his childhood antics.

John and I really didn't make any official plans to expand our family during the next three years because times sure weren't getting any better, but in October, 1935, Bobby came along. Now there was another set of dirty diapers and 2 a.m. feedings to worry about. John was very understanding, though, and again we vowed: "No more children."

Somebody forgot to tell Franklin, however, and shortly after New Year's Day, 1938, he arrived on the scene. I loved Franklin, just as I had loved Sonny and Bobby when they were born, but I've got to admit I was a little disappointed. Like any mother with two precocious boys underfoot, I had wanted a girl the third time around, just to give a little balance to the family.

That's the way the Namath family stayed for a while, and for sure that's the way I wanted us to stay. By 1943 the Depression was over and John was able to work full time again, which made our life a lot easier. Still, it wasn't exactly a comfortable existence I had, and with the United States right in the middle of World War II, I sure didn't feel it was the proper time to add to our already lively household. Twelve years earlier I had

12 married John to ease my work load, but I now found myself running after three wild little boys. Sonny, who early on had found the joys of punching brother Bobby in the nose, was now approaching eleven and had graduated to better things, like throwing rocks through the neighbors' windows. Bobby, having suffered for a while at the hands of Sonny, had discovered that Franklin was an easy target. And Franklin—well, Franklin liked to ride his little bicycle through other people's flower beds and kick strangers in the shins. Already the Namaths had quite a reputation around Beaver Falls, and while the boys were developing, I was too—a good strong right arm in what was usually a futile attempt to keep some kind of order around the house.

Then, just like that, I found out I was going to have still another baby. Okay. By this time everybody in town knew I wanted a girl, and with Sonny, Bobby, and Franklin to ride herd on, I think maybe people were actually feeling a little sorry for me. I knew for sure *I* wanted a change of pace. Of course, I knew there was always the possibility of having another boy, but that was something I didn't even want to think about. This time I was going to have a baby girl, no questions asked. I even took the positive approach and did the new baby's room entirely in pink: a pink crib, pink walls, pink blankets, and pink sweaters. I even made a little pink ribbon for her hair.

Maybe it was out of sympathy, but my doctor agreed with me 100 percent—or at least ninety-nine percent. On May 31, 1943, I went to Dr. James Smith for a checkup and in a completely confident manner he said, "Rose, everything is just fine. I really can't see that little baby of yours arriving for at least another two weeks—and I guarantee you it's going to be a girl." I couldn't have been happier. As I walked home, I could only think about the little girl who would soon be such a welcome addition to our family.

Almost as soon as I reached my front door I began having these terrible pains. Now, I'd had them three times before and I sort of suspected what was going on, but Dr. Smith's absolute and complete confidence that I was at least two weeks away reassured me. After all, Dr. Smith had delivered hundreds of kids and I'd only had three, so what did I know? With no concern at all, I started the week's wash.

A couple of hours later I finished hanging the last of the wet clothes and by then the sun was beating down from directly overhead. Beads of perspiration dripped from my forehead. And the pains—the pains were coming closer and closer. I knew my baby was ready, and no doctor in the world, not even the fine Dr. Smith, was going to tell me, or her, differently.

Nowadays when a woman is ready to have a baby, she gets in a nice car and is driven in relative comfort to the hospital. John and I, however, still didn't have a car. He gathered a few of my night clothes and we began the short walk to Providence Hospital together. Now, I've always enjoyed a short walk—the hospital, over on Third Avenue, was only three blocks away from our house—but this was different. John had been through births before, too, and he realized our baby could be born at any minute. We moved along with him half-running and half-pulling me by the arm. It wasn't exactly a Sunday stroll.

This wasn't my first trip to Providence Hospital. It was my second. The first was to visit a sick friend. All three of my other children had been born at home, right in my bedroom. This was going to be a new experience, which was fine with me, because I thought little girls deserved something special.

An experience it certainly was. John and I barely got through the front door when two attendants saw what was happening—or what was about to happen—and grabbed me away from my husband and pulled me along the corridors into the maternity ward. Meanwhile, Dr. Smith had arrived and was busily scrubbing his hands and slipping on his rubber gloves. Finally, he was ready, and so was I. Just a few minutes later I heard those old familiar words: "It's a boy!" Talk about being shocked.

When the nurse brought my baby to me, wrapped in a blue blanket, I don't think I was in any condition to do a *Czardas*—that's a Hungarian folk dance—but I would have been less than human if I hadn't been excited about that first peek, even if my thoughts still were a little pink. But when I peeled back the blanket and looked at his face, my first words were, "Oh, no. This couldn't be mine." He did have those Namath dimples—all the brothers have them—but his long, black hair and his dark skin made him look more Spanish than Hungarian. But when he opened his blue green eyes and stretched his mouth into a wonderful little smile (I know newborn babies aren't supposed to smile, but this one did), I knew that this good-looking baby was mine.

I had always liked the name Joseph, and since he had been born on his grandfather William Bartus's birthday, his father and I baptized him Joseph William Namath.

At first, Joey didn't want to feed. I tried all sorts of various formulas, but he kept his mouth firmly shut. (Not too much later I realized what a rare condition this was for him.) Finally, I heated up some milk and put a secret ingredient in it, and from that time on he was a precious little angel. No, no matter what Joey says now, that secret ingredient wasn't Johnny Walker Red, it was just plain sugar.

However, I do admit to giving Joey his first taste of the hard stuff. He began cutting teeth when he was about nine months old, and his gums were so tender he just cried and cried from the pain. I took out a special bottle of clear liquid we always kept around the house and rubbed some on his gums. From that day on there was never any problem. He turned into a marvelous baby, always so happy and playful. I think that maybe even today when Joey gets a toothache, a stiff shoulder, or a sore leg, he might occasionally take a sip of our old magic potion.

Shortly after Joey was born, we Namaths moved to the house where, as it turned out, we would stay the longest, at 802 Sixth Street in Beaver Falls, not far from the corner of Seventh Avenue. Now, with four sons around, our household was certainly full enough, and John and I again promised not to have any more children. This was finally one promise we kept, but as the years went by we still both felt that something was missing from our lives—a little girl.

And so in 1949, six years after Joey was born, we made plans to adopt a girl. In Beaver Falls there was the cutest twelve-year-old girl—just a month older than Franklin—who came from a broken home, and it just seemed as though God intended for her to be mine. She lived with us for six months before the courts saw how much she needed us and how much John and I needed her, and it wasn't long before her name was officially changed to Rita Namath. Finally, I had a daughter, and John and I found a love and understanding for her that couldn't have been deeper if I had given her life myself. Now, at last, our family was complete.

Rita was good for everyone. She was Franklin's age, but she also got along well with Sonny and Bobby. The two older boys had to like her if for no other reason than she was great at rock fighting, a big item among the kids of Beaver Falls. She could manage Franklin because she wasn't afraid to pop him in the nose when he got out of line. And as for baby Joey, he quickly learned about the joys and pitfalls of having an older sister.

Now our family numbered seven, and it finally seemed as though life was smiling on us. I certainly didn't have any less work to do, but as Rita got older she pitched in around the house, just as I had around mine when I was growing up. I thought the Namath story was moving along quite nicely, and I also thought I knew the ending. I felt all my kids would eventually grow up, someday have families of their own, and live quiet, uneventful lives. But even as Joey learned to walk and then to run, it wasn't hard to tell that behind those sleepy eyes, eyes that had already lost their blue and turned a beautiful shade of green, lurked a little boy who longed for exciting adventure.

Still, I couldn't have realized that with Joey's birth the most dramatic part of the Namath family story was just beginning.

TWO

I n a flash it seemed as though the smell of baby powder was gone forever—and all the other smells, too, that come with raising a big family—and that my youngest, Joey, was following in the footsteps of his older brothers in search of mischief and adventure. Even after the war I guess you'd have to say that we Namaths still weren't exactly well-to-do. To somebody passing by, I suppose our home on Sixth Street, a two-story frame house, looked like a place Archie Bunker might have lived in before he moved to New York City, but it was no better or no worse than the majority of homes in Beaver Falls. I don't really think that Joey, like most kids raised in his circumstances, ever really understood that his family wasn't what you'd call uptown. After all, Beaver Falls provided everything a little boy needed: a river, the woods, little street gangs, all sorts of mysterious places to explore, and even garbage cans to tip over in the early morning hours. And in the immediate neighborhood were such niceties as a junkyard, a factory or two, an old building that housed the Fame Laundry, and the 7-Up Bottling Company. What more could a precocious youngster in search of real adventure ever ask for?

I really feel that Beaver Falls was just perfect for Joey's personality—and the personalities of all the Namath brood. By the time Joey was ready to strike out on his own, everybody in town knew of the Namaths. With Sonny, Bobby, and Franklin paving the way—and Rita, too, a little while later—you could be sure that whenever something unusual happened in the neighborhood, at least one of my kids was in on it.

Joey made his first real friend when he was about five. Sixth Street wasn't really a main thoroughfare, but I tried to make it clear that Joey wasn't to cross it alone under any circumstances. Once given the challenge, however, he quickly responded. My lecturing did little good, and every time I turned my back I could be sure Joey was off on another mad dash across that street. I soon found out the reason: a little boy named Linwood Alford, who was the same age as Joey and just about the same size. Both of them were as skinny as a rail, and Linny had just about the saddest pair of dark brown eyes I'd ever seen. They really did look alike. Except for one thing: Linny was black. That wasn't really too surprising, because even then the Namaths were one of the few white families in the neighborhood.

When I found out what was going on, I went over to meet Mrs. Alford—her first name was Mary but for some reason I always called her "Mrs. Alford" and she always called me "Mrs. Namath"—and we made arrangements to get the boys safely across the street. From that moment on, Mrs. Alford and I had the time of our lives keeping track of our little protégés. Joey and Linny became inseparable and even today, although each has long since gone his separate way, they manage to keep in touch.

They were so close that Joey even wanted to look like Linny, which he thought to accomplish one day by smearing brown shoe polish all over his face. I quickly put an end to that; I didn't particularly mind Joey wanting to be black, but I sure did mind making him white again afterward. Joey and Linny ate together, worked together, played together, made big plans together, and sometimes even slept together. And woe be it to Mrs. Alford and myself if we dared to keep them apart.

For example, we often made a short day-trip to Massillon, Ohio, to visit my brother Paul and his wife, Mary, and it was always just assumed that Linny was part of the plans. On one particular Sunday, however, he wasn't. John woke up at the crack of dawn and decided on the spur of the moment to make the trip. And believe me, when John decided something, all the rest of us tripped all over ourselves to get on the road. Linny was left behind, and that entire day Joey was just miserable. Even that night on the way home he sobbed and cried that he would never forgive me, until finally he drifted asleep in my arms. I heaved a sigh of relief.

But when we drove into our darkened driveway, on a kind of nice, warm, summery night, I saw the shadowy figure of Linny sitting on our front porch, shading his eyes from the headlights of our car. Even before the car came to a stop, Joey was wide awake and out of my arms.

As Linny walked toward our car, I could see big tears pouring down his cheeks. He looked at Joey with those sad, pathetic brown eyes and cried, "How could you do it, Joey? How could you do it to me?"

"I didn't, I didn't," Joey screamed. "I didn't do it. *They* did it." And he pointed the accusing finger at John and me.

He smeared his tears with his dirty little hands and stuck out his lower lip and sobbed again, "They did it."

Linny glared at me and said, "Mrs. Namath, I'm never gonna f'give you. *Never.*" And with that, the two young boys rushed toward each other sobbing and exchanging hugs as though they had been apart for years. It was a precious moment and one that I'll never forget.

As it turned out, that was just one of many incidents. I guess for a little schoolboy, summer vacation was the best time of the year. To a little boy's mother, however, especially if that little boy happened to be a Namath, that period from June to September was just awful. All I did was count the days until my little boy would be out from underfoot and safely back in the classroom.

Besides, summers in Beaver Falls can be miserably hot. Real dog days. It was especially uncomfortable the summer between Joey's first year at St. Mary's Grammar School and his second, but only part of the discomfort was caused by the weather. Just after school ended for the summer, I saw Joey running up the street bubbling with pride and with beads of sweat dripping from his forehead. He rushed into the house and handed me his report card: "Joseph William Namath has been promoted to the second grade."

"Joey, I am real proud of you," I said. "Now go on up and
change your clothes."

Joey raced for the stairs, slipped on the first step, and fell flat
on his face. He jumped up laughing and ran upstairs. Seconds
later I heard Linny banging on the front door.

"Guess what, Mrs. Namath," he shouted. "I'm goin' to the
second grade."

Just as I finished telling Linny how proud I was of him, too,
Joey came falling down the steps—all fourteen of them—then
bounced up with a "Wow, that hurts," brushed his scraped
elbow, and ran out of the house with Linny close behind.

The door barely banged shut when they were back inside to
make the summer's first raid on the icebox. They grabbed some
lunch meat and some bread and ran out into the sunshine as
the door again slammed hard behind them.

It wasn't even the first official day of vacation, and already I
was dreading the summer. As if keeping track of them after
school and on the weekends wasn't enough. *Edes Istenem,*" I
thought. "Sweet Jesus, have mercy."

Lord, the mischief they could find. One day I found them
playing "doctor" with a little neighborhood girl, but I quickly
revoked their license when they wanted to know why she didn't
have something they had. On another afternoon they climbed
to the roof of the Fame Laundry and hung over the side of the
two-story building just laughing at Mrs. Alford and me as we
begged and pleaded for them to come down. On a third
afternoon big brother Franklin chose to make manservants out
of the little boys, much to their dismay and Franklin's glee. And
the summer was barely beginning.

Then things quieted down for three weeks, which only
served to make me more nervous. I had already learned that
silence from those two only meant more trouble was brewing,
and the tension in the air was like Dodge City at high noon.
Then one especially hot afternoon, the kind where all you
ought to have to do is sit on the front porch and fan yourself
and drink lemonade, just when I thought we all had made it
safely through another day, I suddenly heard Mrs. Alford
scream, "Lordy, Lordy, Lordy."

From the tone of her voice I thought for sure the Seventh
Trumpet had just sounded. I looked out the kitchen window

and saw Mrs. Alford running up the narrow alley next to our house, pointing to the sky, and shouting all the time, "Lordy, Lordy, Lordy."

Then, like a ton of bricks, it hit me: the railroad trestle. The trestle connected two hills near the neighborhood and was used by freight trains carrying supplies to one of the mills. Had there been an accident? Not likely, since at its highest point the trestle stood 100 feet above a cluster of a dozen or so homes in the valley below, and I was sure I would have heard a derailment. Was somebody *on* the trestle? That could be dangerous, because if a train did come along, there would be no place to go except over the side.

All of this flashed through my mind in a split second as I watched Mrs. Alford high-stepping up the alley. Then I heard the low, familiar moan of a train whistle and hurried onto the back porch. I looked up and saw two kids hanging from beneath the trestle, the long freight train rumbling not more than a foot over their heads.

I turned to Rita, who had been playing near the house, and said, "If those little guys were mine, I'd give them the beating of their lives."

"Mom," said Rita, "put on your glasses and take a good look."

Now there were two of us high-stepping up the alley shouting, "Lordy, Lordy, Lordy. Don't let them fall."

In a moment, half the town had gathered. It seemed like an eternity before the train finally passed to the other hillside and Joey and Linny—who else?—were able to stretch and struggle and pull themselves up to safety. No one was able to say a word. We all just stared and shook our heads as they quickly climbed down and ran over to us.

"Hey, mom," said Joey. "Did you see that? We almost got killed."

Later that night Joey got his first taste of the safety blitz. It was obvious my husband John had been informed of the day's events, and he stormed into the house huffing and puffing like a mad bull. Leave it to Joey to say casually, "Hi, dad. Somethin' wrong?"

Just a little bit. Joey got a good spanking out of that, but it wasn't his first and it wouldn't be his last. The little fellow took it all in stride. Then he rubbed his grubby little hand under his nose and wiped the tears from his dirty face and very noncha-

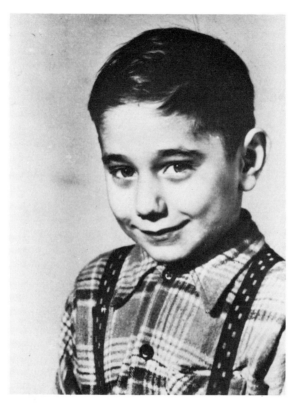

Joey Namath, age six, already has the twinkle of mischief in his green eyes.

Opposite page: Top—Joey, wearing his favorite overalls, poses with an unidentified friend. Bottom—(L-R) Brothers Franklin, Bobby, and John, with Joey riding high.

Top left—(Back Row, L-R) Franklin and Bobby Namath, Grandmother Rose Juhasz, Cousin Barbara Lee Juhasz, and John Namath. (Front Row, L-R) Rita Namath, Cousins Corinne Molnar and Paul Samuel Juhasz, and Joey.

Top right—Grandfather Alexander Juhasz and young Joey. Bottom— The Namath family poses for a fun shot with (L-R) Rose, Franklin, John (standing), the father John, Rita, and Joey at the wheel.

Opposite page: Top—Joey's grandparents Alexander and Rose Juhasz. Bottom—Joe's mother, Rose Juhasz, at age four months.

Right—Rose as a young mother of five children. Bottom—Rose's brothers, the late Joe Juhasz and Paul Juhasz. Joe was the godfather of Joey Namath.

Top—Joe Namath's boyhood home in Beaver Falls, Pa. Bottom—Joey (center) and John with their father John Namath.

Opposite page: Top left— It's a cold Pennsylvania day for (L-R) Rita, Franklin, a cousin, Barbara Lee Juhasz, and Joey in front. Top right—Joey's best pal and partner in assorted business- es, Linny Alford. Bottom— The frame building in the center was the home of Linny Alford.

Joey in his favorite red wagon.

Opposite page: Top—Joey Namath, age eight. Bottom—Joey, first row, third from the left, takes his first Communion.

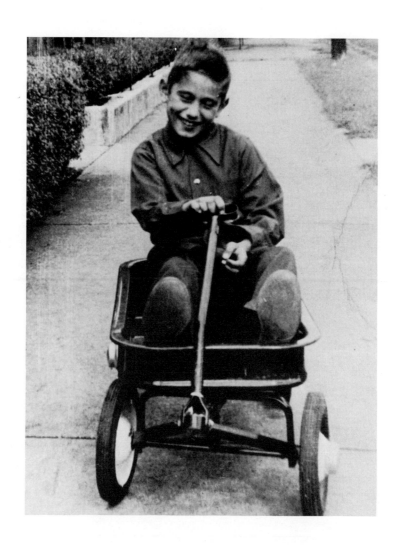

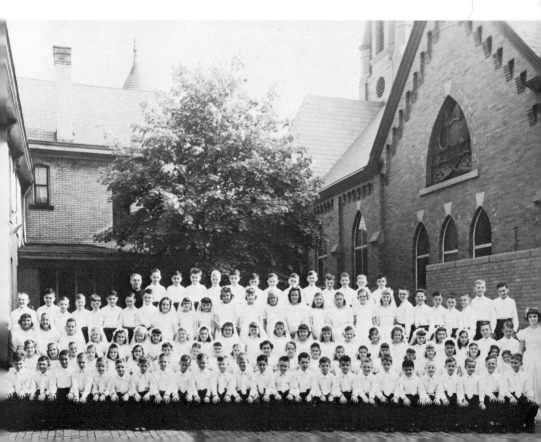

Top—The undefeated 1960 Beaver Falls Tigers had plenty of rabid supporters. Bottom—Joe, in his early teens, sported a flat top haircut, as he did still in his later teens.

Beaver Falls News-Tribune

Beaver Falls News-Tribune

Top left—Joe (No. 14) was already a star on his junior high basketball team. Top right—Snappy one-handed shots and fancy-dan passes were Joe's undoing on the Beaver Falls varsity basketball team. Bottom—(L-R) Rose's father, Alexander Juhasz, Rose, John, and his father John Namath.

Top—Beaver Falls Junior High School where Joe Namath began his football apprenticeship. Bottom—Beaver Falls High School which Joe was to lead to the Western Pennsylvania Football Championship.

Top—This junkyard was a prize customer of Namath-Alford Enterprises. Bottom—This wagon was the essential vehicle in the Namath-Alford Enterprises.

Top—Rose Szolnoki with her
eighteen grandchildren. Bottom
left—Rose on her way to Mass.
Bottom right—Bobby Namath and
his wife, Billie.

*Top—Joe Namath wears No. 17 on the front row of the
junior high team. Bottom—Joe has graduated to the high
school varsity team and to No. 19.*

Top left—A rare photograph of Joe Namath, power hitter and pitcher, who was to turn down a $20,000 baseball bonus after high school. Top right—Joe remains his cool self, wearing sunshades in the team baseball picture. Bottom left—The only known photograph of Joe Namath making a tackle as a defensive halfback before he could make the Beaver Falls team as the quarterback.

lantly asked, "Hey, what's for supper?" as though nothing at all had happened.

The next several days after what became known as the "trestle incident" passed uneventfully. This was the summer of 1950 and Sonny, the oldest boy, had already graduated from high school and was in Korea with the U.S. Army, but with Bobby, Franklin, Rita, and Joey still underfoot, the calm was always like being in the eye of a hurricane. The three older kids played baseball or devised various forms of adolescent mischief, while Joey and his friend Linny amused themselves with cowboys and Indians or sockball—in which you fill an old sock full of older socks and use it as a softball, football, or almost any other kind of ball.

Later that summer I was chatting in the yard with Mrs. Alford about how peaceful life had become. But as usual, we'd spoken too soon, for suddenly a piercing scream ripped through the neighborhood and a second later we saw Joey turn the corner and head for home, all the while glancing over his shoulder with a look of absolute terror in his eyes. Then, predictably, there was another scream as Linny dashed homeward around the same corner. They were both trembling so much they could barely speak.

"We were playin' boat," Joey stammered, "and Linny got a dead man in his."

"Yeah," Linny said, "and he ain't movin' or doin' nothin'. Just layin' dead."

"But," Joey added, "the dead guy said, 'I'm gonna get you.'"

Boat? A talking dead man? I couldn't figure it out. But knowing Joey and Linny, I realized anything was possible, even the talking dead.

"Come on," I said. "Show me where you play boat."

They were reluctant, but with Mrs. Alford and me dragging them by the arms, they directed us to the Roy Powell Funeral Home just around the corner on Seventh Street. They showed us around back, where there was a garage and the entrance to a cellar.

"In there," Joey said, pointing to the cellar door. "That's where we play boat."

It was more curiosity than bravery that took me inside. It was cool and damp in the cellar, and the only light came from the open door behind me and two bleak windows. I saw four empty caskets in a row, and beyond them a fifth casket on an elevator ready to be carried up to the parlor. Now things began to make sense. Joey and Linny had played "boat" by climbing into the four empty caskets. But the fifth casket, the one in the elevator, had an occupant and like Linny had said, he wasn't "movin' or doin' nothin'. Just layin' dead."

That took care of the first half of the mystery, but the part about the talking dead man wasn't cleared up until a few days later when I saw Mr. Powell himself. Mr. Powell usually had that sad, sympathetic look all undertakers seem to have, but on this afternoon he was almost bursting with laughter.

"Rose, come here a minute," he said. "Did you know that Joey and Linny have been visiting my cellar?"

I had to admit that I did.

"Well, the other day I was working on a body in one of the caskets—final touches, you know—when Joseph and Linwood came in. They hadn't seen me, so I sort of eased down behind the casket to see what they were up to. They came over to the casket with the body in it and I just couldn't resist. I could see they were already plenty frightened, but I thought I would add just a little bit of drama. When they peeked in, I moaned in a deep voice, 'I'm going to get you.' Well, you never saw two bigger pairs of eyes in your life, and they tripped all over each other trying to get out. I don't think either one of them will be back for a while."

By now Mr. Powell was almost doubled over with laughter and I was, too. It was one of the few times Joey and Linny ever got a real comeuppance and, believe me, it was long overdue.

During those hot summer nights, Joey and Linny would often sleep together on our front porch. They would climb into one sleeping bag, huddle close together, and drift off to sleep. But never for very long. First, the screen door would slam. Then I'd hear an "Ouch!" as Linny stubbed his toe on the living room sofa. Then there would be a "bang, clatter, clunk" as Joey dropped a pan or two in the kitchen. And, finally, another loud slam as the screen door banged shut once again. The fresh summer air must have given the boys a tremendous appetite because the cycle was as continuous as it was predictable: slam . . . "Ouch!" . . . bang, clatter, clunk . . . slam.

One morning, the banging, slamming, and pounding was even louder than usual. It sounded like a small war, in fact. I got up, blew out the candle beside my statue of St. Mary, and sneaked down the steps. I peered silently in the grey, misty morning onto the front porch. Joey and Linny were construct- ing a small box, and it was obvious they were about to go into the shoeshine business. I didn't say a word. Bootblacking seemed constructive enough, and who knows? The two of them might even make a few pennies.

They obviously had the same idea.

"I'm gonna buy an airplane with the money I make," I heard Joey say.

"I'm gonna buy a big Caddy," added Linny. "You like yellow and purple Caddies, Joey?"

"Yeah, people can really see those colors. And I'm gonna buy Mom a new house, too."

When they finished their box, they slung it between them on two straps and headed off towards the unsuspecting populace of Beaver Falls, their steps high and proud like winning trotters. In a few minutes they were far down Sixth Street and out of sight.

By early afternoon there was no sign of the boys, much to my surprise. Joey's and Linny's lunchtime appearances were as regular as an alarm clock; becoming millionaires was one thing, but I never figured they'd pass up food along the way. Later in the day on my way to the grocery store, I noticed a man feverishly trying to wipe something off his feet. He took several very careful steps, and it was then I noticed that his shoes, although old, were freshly polished —along with his cuffs and socks.

Later, as I left the supermarket, I noticed that the clerk's shoes were unusually clean and shiny, and also that there was a big glob of brown shoe polish stuck to his light green trousers. And on the way home—it was only a three-block walk—I must have noticed ten pairs of newly polished shoes, as well as ten pairs of newly polished cuffs and socks.

Thus Namath & Alford Enterprises got off to a rocky start. Joey and Linny hadn't made quite enough to buy that airplane and yellow and purple Caddy, but other business opportunities quickly came their way. They sold fishing worms for a while until they made the mistake of storing their surplus in my icebox. They sold lemonade on a street corner, quickly drank up their profits, then relocated to one of the hot mills, where the sweltering heat of August and the two thousand-degree temperatures of the blast furnaces combined to create a powerful thirst in the men who worked there. Business boomed until the foreman realized it was a little too dangerous for two kids to be running around a foundry. They went into the bottle-collecting business, getting two cents for a pop bottle and a nickel for a milk jug, until Rita discovered they were playing a sort of con game. Joey would go to the front door of a house and keep whoever answered occupied until Linny could run around to the back and run off with the bottles.

However, Joey had an explanation which I found hard to argue with. "Some people gave us the bottles, some said we couldn't take them, and some people said they didn't have any," he said. "If they said we couldn't take any, we didn't. But if they said they didn't have any and Linny found some out back, then we took 'em, 'cause they were lyin'."

They were walking a fine line, but the more I think about it now, the more I feel Joey may have been in the right. Even to this day Joey hates people who lie, and I don't think he's ever told a lie himself.

So Namath & Alford Enterprises, Bottle-Collecting Division, went out of business, too. But, as I found out, it's hard to keep a good corporation down. One day near the end of summer I had the boys clean out the cellar and told them to haul the junk to the dump in Linny's small wagon. Just then, an old junkman with a rickety, horse-drawn wagon made his way up the street shouting, "Scrap and rags. I buy scrap and rags." He stopped in front of our house to talk with Joey and Linny, and from the window I watched as the boys threw their junk onto the wagon.

Immediately they raced in with the news that they had fast-talked the junkman into taking their junk. "He even paid us for it," Joey announced proudly.

That was the start of Namath & Alford Enterprises, Junk Dealers. For the next several days the boys got up early and took off for Lord knows where in search of stuff to collect and sell. It was hard work, and it often took them two or three days to get up a load big enough to offer the old man. And always there were the negotiations.

"I give you twenty cents, no penny more," the old man would say.

Then Joey and Linny would huddle several feet away and come back with a counteroffer. "Twenty-five."

"No, no, no. I give you twenty-two. No more."

Once again there would be a hurried conference. "Okay, okay," Joey and Linny would say. "You win. We'll settle for twenty-five."

And the old man would give the boys a quarter. I suspect he enjoyed those "negotiations" a lot more than the few pennies' profit he might have made.

But they got their just deserts. After a while I noticed that the boys' profits were way up, although they were putting in less and less time making their rounds. I did a little detective work, and early one morning I saw Joey and Linny come down the street with a full load of junk, although they'd been out for only a few minutes. And, I noticed, the junk they were hauling looked awfully familiar; it was the same load they'd sold the day before.

I went to the back door and listened as the boys struggled and grunted with their collection. And I also heard Linny say, "Boy, Joey, that sure was a neat idea. We sold him this load four times already."

Well, right at that moment Namath & Alford Enterprises came to an abrupt end. And so did the summer of Joey's seventh year.

Probably the only time of the year I really enjoyed doing the wash was when I had to get the kids ready for school. That was a sign somebody else would soon have to try and ride herd on Joey and Linny five days a week for nine straight months. A three-month stint was about all Mrs. Alford and I could take.

The school clothes for the boys were stored in the attic in boxes marked with the numbers 1 through 12, each number indicating a school grade. With Sonny already out of high school and in the army, I now only had to get out boxes 11 (for Bobby), 8 (for Franklin), and 2 (for Joey). Rita had her own clothes, of course, but considering her tomboyishness, she probably could have been outfitted from the boys' boxes as well. Although the boys' clothes were old, they were always neat and well fitted. I was good with a needle and thread. Sometimes I'd let out a little of the cuff, other years I'd take in a little, and when the clothes got to where they needed three patches, they became play clothes. Most items, though, lasted twelve years and served all four boys.

Then there were the shoes. When Bobby finished with them, since he was the second son, they always needed retreading. But the shoe shops in Beaver Falls always did such a good job that Franklin could add his twenty thousand miles and still leave enough for Joey's twenty-five. And then, horrors, it would be summer again.

The years of Joey's childhood fled by so quickly that sometimes I still can't believe they are long gone, although there were plenty of times during the days of Namath & Alford Enterprises when I stared at the hands of a clock and they never seemed to move at all. There were more adventures, more futile attempts to keep Joey in line, more of those blessed Septembers when school started, and more of those terrible Junes when school let out.

All in all, I think Joey spent a wonderful and memorable childhood. It was certainly memorable for me. For sure we weren't the richest family in town, and at times it even seemed as though the whole world was against us. I don't think Joey was ever really aware of that, however. He wasn't special in that respect, because I believe all kids have a certain innocence which they don't lose until their teens, no matter how "street smart" they're forced to become.

Most important of all, though, in Joey's formative years, was his friendship with Linny Alford. I don't think two closer buddies ever lived. I remember one time when two neighborhood bullies jumped Joey a couple of blocks from home and began beating on him. Linny was home at the time watching television, and he couldn't have seen the fight start or even have heard Joey's screams for help. But for some unknown reason, he knew Joey was in trouble and raced out to the rescue. It was a strange sort of ESP that developed entirely because of their deep friendship.

There is one other little item about Joey and Linny worth mentioning. Beginning when they were both about ten, they became members of the best sandlot football team in the world—or at least in Beaver Falls, Pennsylvania. There were a total of three neighborhood teams in the city. The "rich" white kids made up one, the poor black kids from the "wrong" side of

the tracks made up another, and the third team was composed
of Joey at quarterback, Linny at what I guess you'd call
scatback, and nine other little black kids. Their record in the
first year of their franchise was something like 112 wins and no
defeats against all comers. I know the Pittsburgh Steelers and
the New York Jets have great teams, but it takes one heckuva
ball club to play a game every day after school and six more on
the weekends and still go undefeated. I sometimes saw their
games, which were played on that dirt athletic field behind the
high school, but I had no premonitions of things to come.

Linny summed up their greatness to me when he said, "You
see, Mrs. Namath, the white guys up on the hill got the passing
and the smarts, but they ain't got speed. The guys from across
the tracks got all the speed, but not too much smarts, and ain't
none of those guys gonna throw the ball. Now, *we* got the
speed, *we* got the smarts, and *we* got the man—Joey. Ain't no
one gonna outrun us up on the hill, and ain't no one gonna
outthink us or outpass us across the tracks. We're the best."

And they were.

As Joey moved through St. Mary's Grammar School, he
quickly learned, if he didn't sense it already, that the Namath
clan was quite famous among the good sisters. As Joey tells it in
his own book, *I Can't Wait Until Tomorrow . . . 'Cause I Get
Better-Looking Every Day*, when he entered the seventh grade a
teacher asked, "Joey, are you related to Franklin Namath?"

"Yes, ma'm," Joey answered politely.

"Are you related to Bobby Namath?"

"Yes, ma'm."

"And Sonny Namath . . . are you related to him, too?"

"Yes, ma'm. They're my brothers."

By now Joey was positively bubbling over with pride that this
teacher knew all his older brothers.

"Well, you just get your books and move right up front next
to me," the teacher said. "I know all about the Namaths."

Right then and there Joey told me, "Aw, mom. Everybody
picks on me." It was something he would say often over the
next few years. I wonder why.

Joey was the last of the Namaths; he had a lot to live up to
and sometimes a little to live down. Sonny, the oldest, spent the
first years of his childhood during the Depression, when kids
grew up quickly. It didn't take Sonny long to find out that a

strong back and a tight fist were the necessities of life. Black eyes and bloody noses were routine and Sonny, like most kids his age, believed it was better to give than to receive. Sonny always seemed to be going around straightening everything out, "just for the record." And just for the record, I went around trying to straighten out Sonny.

Bobby, too, learned all the devilish tricks of childhood, and after him, Franklin and Rita. They have all turned out well and I couldn't be prouder of the way the members of my family conducted themselves through good times and bad, but for a few years there I was a familiar face around the offices of the various school principals. I recall with particular amusement the day Sonny, Bobby, Franklin, and Rita (Joey was too young) all got called into the principal's office at once. It was like a family reunion. And it wasn't too long before Joey started upholding the Namath tradition himself.

Joey's preteen years ended on a sad and disruptive note. The same year he entered the seventh grade, 1955, his father and I were divorced. The reasons aren't important to this story, but because of our separation Joey and I were suddenly out on our own. By then, all of his older brothers, as well as Rita, had left home, and now Joey and I had to leave the modest house on Sixth Street where he had grown up. He had to say good-bye to his little pal, Linny, and although they remained close friends, they could no longer just walk across the street into each other's homes. I felt bad for Joey. The next several years were the most trying ones of his life—and mine. It was hard for me to find steady employment. I was only forty-three, but I had spent all of my life raising a family, and good jobs just weren't that easy to come by. We moved around from apartment to apartment, and just when we got settled into one place it seemed as though we would have to move out and look for another. For the most part, people who knew the situation Joey and I were in sincerely tried to be helpful, and they were. But we often ran into cruel individuals who cared only about themselves, like one particular landlord I'll never forget who rented us a house knowing very well it was going to be torn down three weeks later.

It was a struggle, but Joey was a great help to my spirits and somehow we managed. He couldn't possibly have known of all my frustrations, but I think he sensed them. And when he did, he'd always calm me by saying, "Don't worry, Mom. Things will be okay." Looking into those sleepy, mischievous eyes, I just had to believe him.

Joey never once complained about those days, but often I would cry for him. He was my youngest child, the only one living at home, and I loved him with all my heart. If those years were hard for me, I know they were far more difficult for him. But when things were the worst, we always managed to bounce back by eagerly looking forward to the future. Faith in tomorrow is a powerful weapon.

THREE

All of my sons, from Sonny on down through Bobby and Franklin and finally Joey, have the same basic facial features—the Namath dimples, the Namath nose, and the Namath eyes, heavy lidded and full of the devil. And although all four of them now come in a wide assortment of sizes and shapes, every one was a good athlete at Beaver Falls High School. I can't tell you exactly why either, except that maybe growing up in a rough and tough mill town would make a good athlete out of just about anybody. But, as I suggested earlier, I think the reason is a little more complicated than that. If a boy grows up in less than ideal circumstances—and I don't care whether it's on a New York City street corner, in an isolated Appalachian hamlet, or in a mill town—he wants to get out. And there are really only two ways. One is the army, which is the route Sonny took right after he graduated from high school, and the other is college, usually through an athletic scholarship. I don't know exactly whether parents sit down one day and say, "Okay, Joey, here's a football. Go out and get a college education with it," or whether it happens more naturally. But I'll bet that every little boy who has ever grown up poor dreams of an athletic career at some time in his life. Usually those dreams don't work out very well, but sometimes—like in Joey's case—they work out just perfectly.

But the funny thing is, a lot of those same kids who try so hard to leave home end up right back where they started from, just as happy as they can be. Sonny, Bobby, and Franklin all live right here in Beaver Falls, or nearby, and even Joey, after all these years as a big national celebrity, has said he might like to come back some day and settle down in the place where he grew up. Maybe he tells me that just for my benefit, but at least that's what he says.

At any rate, I'm getting a little ahead of my story here. As I said, all of Joey's brothers were good athletes, and each one in turn seemed to be just a little bit better. Sonny, for example, was an offensive lineman on the Beaver Falls High football team, and Leland Shacahern, his coach at the time, said he was "fairly good." Bobby, the next in line, was an excellent baseball and football player, and pretty good at basketball, too. Franklin, the youngest next to Joey, was good enough at baseball for the Baltimore Orioles of the American League to scout him as a bonus prospect. In fact, the Orioles were ready to offer him a contract but his father and I never let him find out about it. We just sat down at the kitchen table one day and decided college was more important. When he learned about it later he was furious, but I think we made the right decision for him. Franklin, in fact, did go to the University of Kentucky on a football scholarship. Although he didn't graduate, he did room for a while with Lou Michaels who, as a member of the Baltimore Colts, was to play an amusing role in the Namath family history a few years later.

Despite the fine athletic tradition his brothers had started, it didn't appear for the longest time as though Joey was going to be able to carry it on. Although the neighborhood football team he and Linny Alford belonged to had won those 112 straight games one year, Joey just seemed to stop growing when he turned eleven—and he wasn't very big to begin with. Three years later when he entered the ninth grade at the Middle School, he was lucky if he weighed 100 pounds and stood five feet tall when he didn't slouch, which he did a lot.

Well, I couldn't have been more surprised the day Joey came home from practice and announced he was the number one quarterback of his junior high team, the Beaver Falls Tiger

Cubs. My Joey? Why, he could hardly see over his center's rear end, and besides, there were two other quarterbacks on the team whom everybody in town was counting on to lead the varsity in a few years, especially one fellow named Jake Lotz.

But then fate started to play a role in Joey's life, as it does in almost everybody's somewhere along the line. Jake broke his arm in preseason practice, and suddenly Joey was thrust into the starting lineup for the Tiger Cubs' first game against Midland. All he did was throw two touchdown passes in the very first period. In the second, he completed a twelve-yard pass to his good friend Tommy Krzemienski that set up a third touchdown as Beaver Falls won easily, 31–0.

In the next game Joey hit Krzemienski with another touchdown pass as the Tiger Cubs nipped the Ambridge Junior High club, and by then the whole community was thinking those little Cubbies might be something to watch in a couple of years. In fact, the local paper, the *News-Tribune,* said the team had "one of the most devastating offenses for a junior high team witnessed in several seasons."

Despite his success at the Middle School, however, Joey suffered a crushing blow the following summer that might have ended his football career forever if he hadn't had a lot of stick-to-itiveness.

Each year the Beaver Falls High Boosters Club sent about fifty of the best varsity prospects to a special preseason summer camp. The coaches selected the players, but the camp was run by the Boosters themselves. Although its only real purpose was to get the kids in shape before the start of official practice, if you weren't selected as one of those fifty, well, you could just forget about football at Beaver Falls.

Joey wasn't selected, but his ninth grade rival, Jake Lotz, was, and he thought a lot about giving up football right then and there. He loved all kinds of sports. He played baseball and basketball and even ran a little track, but the coaches thought he was just too small to be a good high school quarterback. I must admit I had to agree. Joey always said that if he couldn't make it in football, he wanted to be an airline pilot, and although by that summer—the summer of 1958—he had grown an inch and put on another twenty pounds or so, I fully expected my youngest son's career to be spent in a cockpit.

However, Joey had friends around town—although I didn't know it at the time—and one of them was the head varsity football coach, Bill Ross.

Ross was about to start his last year of coaching before moving up to the position of athletic director for the high school, where he's since been a friend and counselor to the hundreds of Beaver Falls athletes who have passed through his doors. He's an imposing man, standing six feet three inches and weighing about 240 pounds, with enormous hands like ham hocks. But behind that imposing exterior is a gentle, even jolly, human being, and a pretty perceptive one, too. In 1958 he saw something in Joey those other coaches must have missed.

"I had watched him as a Little League baseball player," he told me recently, "and he was just great. You couldn't strike him out and you couldn't hit a ball past him. I had coached the three older brothers and they were all big, strong boys. Even though Joe was small and skinny as a sophomore, he had the kind of framework that led me to believe he would develop in time. And when he did, I always said, 'Look out.' With a little height and weight, Joe would be the best Namath brother of them all."

Joey stuck it out his sophomore year and even made the varsity—they must have had an extra uniform around or something. He didn't play very much, though, and when he did it was always when Beaver Falls was ahead by fifty points or behind by fifty points. Not only that, but he was used primarily as a defensive halfback. I don't think they trusted him to throw the ball, or maybe they still felt he couldn't see over his center's fanny. I really didn't like to see him play under those conditions. It was like adding salt to his already wounded pride.

All of that was in the past, though, when Joey's junior season started. The new head coach was a man named Larry Bruno, and he promised great things for his Tigers, as the Beaver Falls varsity was called. Bruno was a native of East Liverpool, Ohio, and after graduating from high school he had gone on to play for Geneva College, where he was good enough to be selected for the 1946 East-West Shrine Game in San Francisco. The Pittsburgh Steelers even offered him a bonus contract of $125, but he was married and already had a child when he left

34   Geneva, and the regular-season salary the Steelers offered him just wasn't enough to make ends meet. Fortunately for Joey he stayed in Beaver Falls to start a very successful teaching and coaching career.

The quarterback situation was pretty confusing that year. Jake Lotz, Joey's rival from the ninth grade, had moved away from town, and Joey himself had put on a few more inches and a few more pounds, but he still wound up being the number two signal caller behind a senior named Rich Niedbala. A lot of people around town, especially Bobby and Franklin, thought Joey was the better of the two, but for Bruno it was a touchy situation. There were even rumors going around town that Niedbala had threatened to quit if he didn't start. I don't know for sure if that's true, but just maybe something convinced Bruno he'd be better off with two quarterbacks, Niedbala and Namath, rather than with just one.

"I had to start with Rich," said Bruno. "He had the experience. I could see Joe was coming on fast, but Niedbala was my man."

Niedbala was a good quarterback. I don't think there's any doubt about that. In fact, he got a scholarship to the University of Miami in Florida and played behind George Mira, who was an all-American Joey's senior year at the University of Alabama. And so Joey was called upon to play a lot of defensive halfback again his junior year. Although he was considered one of the best in the state, on offense he was still number two—until the last game of the season.

But let Coach Bruno tell the story:

"Joe played quarterback off and on his junior year, but he didn't start until the last game of the year, against New Brighton. In fact, I don't think he started even then. Since it was our last game, as I recall I started all seniors. New Brighton wasn't very good that year, but at the end of the first quarter we were only ahead 7–0. In the second quarter, though, I put in next year's team, and when Joe and the other underclassmen took over, the game became a rout. Joe threw a couple of touchdown passes and we won something like 51–6. Our record was only 4–5–1 that year, but I had a hunch we were going to have a very special team the next fall."

I saw that New Brighton game and I remember Joey's first touchdown pass very well, because I couldn't bear to watch it.

When he faded back and the crowd began to roar, I closed my eyes and covered my ears. It took a lot of bravery for me to sneak a peek just as the receiver—Joey's buddy Tom Krzem-ienski—ran into the end zone.

I remember hearing a man sitting next to me ask his buddy, "Who the hell is that No. 19?"

That was Joey's number, but I kept my mouth shut because I had no idea what the question implied. It even sounded a little belligerent.

I heaved a sigh of relief when the other guy answered, "That's young Namath out there. Nice looking ballplayer."

I was relieved. I'd also just had my first experience as a football mother and believe me, as the years went by, it never got any easier.

Just as Bill Ross had predicted, Joey shot up almost overnight. I could easily remember the days when his football gear seemed to weigh more than he did, and he could barely move around in it. But by the fall of 1960 he was well over six feet tall and had fleshed out to a healthy 175 pounds. He wore that No. 19, and for the first time his jersey wasn't all wrinkled and saggy around the chest. At last, he looked like a real football player. Not only could he see over his center, he had to slouch way down just to take the snap.

And my, how he could throw! Now, as I said earlier, I'm no expert and I'm not going into a lot of detail about how to toss a football around. Besides, Joey has already explained the technical aspects of his game in a very nice book called *Joe Namath: A Matter of Style,* written with Bob Oates, Jr. But I do remember that his brothers, Bobby especially, worked out with him for hours on end. Each day Joey seemed to throw that ball a little harder and a little farther, and according to Bill Kushner, who knows a lot about quarterbacking himself, Bobby helped Joey during those long sessions in two very specific ways.

First of all, Bobby saw that Joey had a tendency to take a "false step" when he set himself up to pass. All I know about a false step is that if you take one, you're about to get in trouble, but in football talk it means that when Joey took the snap from center, instead of backpedaling right away into his pocket, he'd first take a quick step toward the line of scrimmage. It was just a wasted motion, and Bobby broke him of that habit in a hurry. Secondly, Bobby taught Joey the "quick release" that's become his trademark. Most quarterbacks, I'm told, throw sort of sidearm and rock back on their right leg, and then they step forward onto their left leg as they release the ball. But Bobby showed Joey how to pivot his body from the waist up—because that's how you generate most of your strength, just like a golfer or a tennis player does—and to release the ball by snapping it quickly over his right ear, just like a baseball catcher would. This allowed him to wait until the absolute last split second before he actually threw a pass, and it gave his receivers just that much more time to break into the open.

Coach Bruno said many times that he never tried to show Joey how to throw a football. "Joey knew that when he came to me," he said. "I never had to teach him to set up, either. Joey could set up quicker and throw better than any other high school quarterback I've ever seen."

What Bruno did teach Joey was magic—literally. Bruno was a part-time magician and firmly believed that the hand was quicker than the eye. He told his running backs to always act like they were carrying the ball even when they weren't, and he told his linemen to always block as though the ballcarrier was coming through their hole even when he wasn't. And he taught his quarterback—Joey—how to hand off to one back, stick his empty hand in another's belly, and make it all look realistic right up until the whistle stopped the play. You know how sometimes when you're watching football on television and the camera follows some guy who turns out not to even have the ball? Well, in the fall of 1960, there was a lot of that going on in the Beaver Valley, and Joey was behind it all.

Sometimes he faked so well he even fooled the referees. This is what one Pittsburgh sportswriter, Brute Kramer of the *Post-Gazette,* wrote after a game:

"To go one step further, Bill Bache, outstanding district football referee who had the head whistle in the New Castle-Beaver Falls battle, calls Namath the best T-formation quarterback he has ever seen in his 25 years of officiating.

"Bache claims there is absolutely nothing this amazing youngster can't do with a football and that his tricky maneuvering in the backfield is one of the prime reasons why this Beaver Falls outfit is so highly rated this year.

"Ask Bruno about this and he merely observes with a twinkle, 'It's sure nice having him on our side.'

"Bache added, 'I assumed five different positions in back of the Beaver Falls backfield trying to catch just exactly who he handed off to, and I'll be darned if he didn't have me a bit bewildered. Imagine the consternation of the New Castle outfit trying to find out who had the ball.'"

But there I go jumping ahead of my story again. The opening game for Beaver Falls in Joey's senior year was against the Midland Leopards. Midland only had an average team—it was pretty much of a basketball school in those days and in fact has sent at least two players, Norm Van Lier and Simmy Hill, to the pros—but I was nervous and worried, even more than usual. But on the first play of the game, Joey using some of that magic Larry Bruno had taught him, faked the ball to Whitey Harris, one of his halfbacks, and held it on his hip and ran sixty yards for a touchdown. I stopped being nervous after that. Joey completed seven of twelve passes for 174 yards; everybody else played well, too, and Beaver Falls won, 43–13.

Something happened after that first game which I think tells you a lot about Joey. On the bus trip back to Beaver Falls, Coach Bruno sat next to Joey and said he wanted to schedule a practice for the next morning, a Saturday, at 10:30. "I know the other players aren't going to like this," he told Joey, "but if you jump up and down and go along, the rest of the players will jump on the bandwagon, too. And here's why I want a Saturday practice. If anybody is injured, we'll find out in a hurry, and if it's more serious than a bump or a bruise, we'll get him to a doctor. We can also go over our mistakes while they're fresh in our minds."

Coach Bruno later told me that there *was* a lot of groaning when he announced the unusual practice, but when Joey stood up and said a Saturday workout was the greatest thing in the world for their team, in a matter of seconds the rest of the players were up and screaming, too. For the rest of the season those Tigers practiced every Saturday, and I think they even got to like it before the year was over.

Next Friday night was more of the same: Beaver Falls 39, Sharon 7. Then came the first real important test of the year on the road against New Castle. The Hurricanes were one of the perennial powers in western Pennsylvania, and this was to be the renewal of a long-standing rivalry that went back to my own childhood. In fact, in 1924 when I was just twelve years old, I remembered those New Castle ruffians beating our Beaver Falls Tigers, 72–0. The series had been discontinued in 1944, but not before New Castle had beaten us nine straight years without giving up a single point. They probably didn't think it was even worthwhile to schedule us, and you can imagine how everybody in town felt when the news came on the radio that our Tigers had won, 39–0, with Joey scoring two touchdowns and completing nine of thirteen passes for 184 yards.

It was the most important victory of the year so far, but when Joey came home late that night, he was his usual cool self. Even in high school—and later in college and in the pros—I could rarely tell whether Joey's team had won or lost just by looking at him, or whether Joey had thrown a lot of touchdown passes or a lot of interceptions. He always gave 100 percent, but he never got upset when he lost or cocky when he won.

The New Castle victory really got Beaver Falls stirred up, but strangely enough I still hadn't seen the team play, an omission I was determined to correct the next weekend when the Tigers hosted Ambridge, another western Pennsylvania powerhouse. I can still remember the excitement of getting ready for that game. Earlier that year I had been remarried to a kind and understanding man named Steve Szolnoki, and he and I, along with Bobby and Franklin, drove out together to Reeves Stadium on the campus of Geneva College, where the high school played its home games.

Reeves Stadium was actually one of the prettiest spots in Beaver Falls. The field ran north-south, and to the north you could see up a hill to the main campus of the college. To the west were the home stands, where we sat, built right into another hillside. These stands tapered down to an ash and gravel 440-yard running track that surrounded the football field. The east stands were smaller—the whole stadium could probably seat ten or twelve thousand people very comfortably—and behind those stands was a huge parking lot. And behind the parking lot were maybe a dozen railroad tracks going to and from the mills. Occasionally the roar of the crowd competed with the rumble of a passing freight. Finally, off beyond the south goal was a red glow from the Steel Furnaces. Even with all those sights and sounds, though, all I could see were those Beaver Falls Tigers in their orange and black uniforms and my son, the quarterback, in No. 19.

I picked a great night to see Joey play. Early in the game he rolled out to his left and was tackled high and low by the Ambridge defense. Joey was the last to get up from the pile of players, and he held his left shoulder in obvious pain. In a terrible display of sportsmanship, the Ambridge side of the stands cheered. Although Beaver Falls won again, 25–13, Joey only completed three of fifteen passes, his worst night ever as a high school player.

The next morning Joey went to the team doctor, who gave him the bad news. Joey had separated his shoulder and, the doctor said, was through for the season. Joey couldn't believe it. He and his father went to see Coach Bruno, who didn't *want* to believe it, and sent Joey to an orthopedic specialist in town. The specialist examined Joey carefully and then wrapped his shoulder tightly with athletic tape. That could have been the end of Joey's high school career, but he just shrugged the whole thing off and kept going.

By then, of course, Joey had established himself overwhelmingly as the team's leader, both by his skill and his confidence. In that Ambridge game, for example, he nursed a bad ankle the entire night—and he was the team's punter. In a crucial third down and long yardage situation before he hurt his shoulder, Coach Bruno called time out and brought Joey over to the sidelines.

"Joey," he said, "if we have to punt, are you going to be able to kick with your bad ankle?"

"We're not gonna have to punt," Joey retorted, and true to his word, he completed a fifty-four-yard pass on the very next play that set up the first Beaver Falls touchdown.

The season moved right along after the Ambridge game, and Joey and his teammates just kept getting better and better. They defeated Butler, 26–6. They bumped off Farrell, 33–18. And they swamped Aliquippa, 34–7, as Joey had his best night ever, completing fourteen of eighteen passes for 244 yards and three touchdowns. That made the Beaver Falls High record 7–0, and suddenly our very own Tigers were contenders for the championship of western Pennsylvania.

Here's how it all worked out. Beaver Falls played in the Class AA district of the Western Pennsylvania Interscholastic Athletic League, and going into the eighth weekend of the season, there were just two undefeated teams, Beaver Falls and Monessen, and both had just one more district game left. If they both won, there would have to be a playoff for the WPIAL title. But Beaver Falls easily defeated Ellwood City, 26–0, and the same night Monessen got upset by McKeesport, 19–0. That took care of everything, and just to make the season complete, Beaver Falls defeated New Brighton, another traditional rival, 40–6, in the last game of the season to finish with a perfect 9–0 record.

The night of the New Brighton game the whole town of Beaver Falls just went wild. It was the first time anybody could remember that Beaver Falls had gone undefeated and won the WPIAL championship, and everybody in town was bubbling over. And I, of course, was especially proud of Joey—for about twenty-four hours.

It seems that Coach Bruno had promised the boys new football jerseys if they won the championship, as souvenirs of their fine season, but in the end the school budget won out, and poor Mr. Bruno had to say no. But someone on the team—I wonder who—got the bright idea of breaking into the equipment room and "borrowing" them.

Joey may have been a great quarterback and I was certainly proud of that, but he was also an occasional hell-raiser, right up to the end of his high school days. For every touchdown pass he threw, he seemed to get intercepted by various authorities ranging from his mother to his teachers to the Beaver Falls police. One rainy Sunday a few of the boys wanted to relax by playing a little basketball and thought nothing of breaking into the high school gym—after all, nobody was using it—until the police intervened. Then there was the time a car dealership in town, Sahli Chevrolet, put up a big, helium-filled balloon as part of a special sales promotion. Well, it seemed as though Larry Patterson, Whitey Harris, and good old Joey decided that the big balloon would look nice hanging from the high school flagpole with "Take 'em Tigers" painted all over it. Larry, Whitey, and Joey got as far as the roof of Sahli Chevrolet before the good old police appeared again, and all of a sudden three members of the best Beaver Falls High School football team in history were on their way to jail.

Joey never did understand why he was able to find so much trouble. "Aw, Mom," he said, picking up his old refrain, "everybody's always picking on me."

Joey's performances on the basketball court weren't nearly as successful as his gridiron exploits. The coach was a very nice man named Nate Lippe, who, I understand, had some fine high school teams back in the 1940s. He had been retired since 1943, though, until Beaver Falls brought him back for the 1960–61 season. His idea of sound basketball was to slow things down and then take a two-handed set shot. That might have worked twenty years ago, but the kids on his present team had a few other ideas. They liked to pretend they were the Harlem Globetrotters or somebody, and they used a lot of razzle-dazzle and behind-the-back passes and things like that. Before long it was pretty clear poor Mr. Lippe was in for a long season.

For him I guess it was, but for Joey everything came to an abrupt end late in the season against Farrell, a powerful team that went on to win the state championship that year. Midway through the third quarter, Coach Lippe decided that Joey and another player named Benny Singleton were razzling and dazzling just a little bit too much for their own good and promptly benched them. The next thing I knew, Joey had stormed out of the gym with Benny right behind him. I thought they were just going to get a drink of water, but a few minutes later Joey and Benny reappeared in their street clothes, permanently retired from the roundball sport. It was probably for the best.

All during that winter and into the following spring, college coaches and scouts swarmed all over Beaver Falls. Their main target was Joey, but they were after a lot of other players on that 1960 Beaver Falls team as well. Eleven of them, eight starters and three second stringers, eventually received scholarships. I didn't see everything that went on because Coach Bruno handled most of the early negotiations for all the players, but it was pretty clear, even to me, that Joey was something special when *Scholastic Coach* selected him for its all-American team. He had good company on that team, players like Dick Butkus, Ernie Koy, and John Huarte, as well as two other fellows who wound up being very important college rivals of Joey's—Jimmy Sidle and Tucker Frederickson. In Frederickson's case, the rivalry extended right into the pros.

Pretty soon Joey started making all sorts of visitations to places like Arizona State, Michigan State, Indiana, Miami of Florida, Minnesota, Notre Dame, and many other schools as well. Being a good Catholic, I sort of had a preference for Notre Dame. All of my sons were altar boys, even Joey, until he decided it interfered too much with football practice. But when Joey came back from South Bend he said, "Mom, I really like the priests and everything else about the school, but I think I'm gonna look around."

Then I heard him mutter under his breath, "Dang, there aren't any girls there."

Now, I know Joey was only interested in getting a good education and playing football, but he somehow always managed to bring up the importance of "extracurricular" activities. Joey wasn't really a ladies' man in high school, not by a long shot, but I do think it was in the back of his mind that he'd like to go to a place where he'd at least have a fighting chance. And so, the search went on for a school that would provide him with a good education, a good football program, and a few "extracurriculars."

Among the schools Joey visited was the University of Maryland, and upon his return all he could do was rave about somebody named "Hatchet."

"Who's that?" I asked.

"It's a guy named Al Hassan," he said. "He's from New Castle, a really great guy who's the manager of the football team."

"Now, Joey, you know I don't like name-calling. If Al's name is Al, you should call him Al, not Hatchet."

Mainly because of his friendship with Al, Joey finally decided to attend Maryland. But there was one hitch. Maryland required a score of 750 on the Scholastic Aptitude Test, the one that all high school seniors must take, and Joey had scored only 730 the first time around. He had to take the test over. That summer, Al became Joey's unofficial tutor. Every night the two young men would clean up, splash on some Old Spice, and take off, Joey said, to study. Sometimes I wondered what they meant by "study," but when August rolled around, Joey was deadly serious about that SAT. So was Al, who by this time I had come to call Hatchet myself, because he never did answer to his first name.

Hatchet called Joey with the bad news the day after the test: Joey had missed that 750 cutoff by three points. He was terribly disappointed and dragged himself around the house for days not knowing what to do. He got so desperate he even began thinking about Notre Dame again, girls or no girls.

I should point out right here that Joey has always had a good
mind. His teachers from grammar school right up through
high school all said he had a very high IQ and could have been
an excellent student if he had only applied himself in the
classroom the way he did on the football field. He never failed
anything, but he never got A's either. I guess Joey knew long
before the rest of us that football was going to be his life. Being
a really top student didn't make all that much difference to him.
However, here it was late August, and it suddenly looked as
though Joey didn't have much of a future in the classroom or
on the football field.

Things were going on behind the scenes, though, and three
days after Joey found out he couldn't attend Maryland, an
assistant coach from the University of Alabama, by the name of
Howard Schnellenberger, paid us a visit. It seems that Tom
Nugent, the head coach of Maryland, had called his old friend
Paul "Bear" Bryant, the head coach of Alabama, and told him
about Joey. I'm sure Coach Nugent acted out of a sincere desire
to help Joey, but maybe, just maybe, he also wanted to make
sure Joey played for a school Maryland didn't have on its
schedule the next three or four years.

I started piecing that together much later. For now I was
mainly interested in the name Bear Bryant. It sounded so
mean. As Coach Schnellenberger described the Alabama football program, I listened quietly as long as I could. Finally, I just
couldn't resist. "Tell me something," I asked. "How did Coach
Bryant get the name 'Bear'?"

"Well, when Paul wasn't even a teenager yet he wrestled a
bear to the ground and beat 'im," Coach Schnellenberger said,
"and ever since then the name's stuck."

"Is Bear—I mean, Mr. Bryant—a pretty tough man?"

"Well, ma'm, if Coach Bryant's men don't toe the line, he
whups 'em right back into place just like he whupped that
bear."

Right then and there I knew where *I* wanted Joey to go to
school. As you know by now, Joey sometimes had that mischievous tendency to step out of line, and I think he had the notion
that college was going to be four more years of fun and games.
I was relieved to know the University of Alabama and Coach
Bryant might be able to change his mind. Bear Bryant, I could
tell, was definitely my kind of man.

"Alabama *is* where you want to go, isn't it?" I asked Joey.

"When do I report?" he said. Joey was really getting excited.

Coach Schnellenberger smiled. "We're goin' south together, and I'm just about ready to leave."

And that's the way it was. We all rushed around madly for the next few hours trying to get Joey ready. Joey and I dashed into town to fix him up with a wardrobe of sorts, and everybody else pitched in, too. Franklin even helped pack his suitcases. I think he wanted to get Joey on his way before he changed his mind.

In the space of those few hours, Joey's childhood came to an end, and I even sensed it was time to stop calling him "Joey." (I still do though, even today.) I realized for the first time that I had no more family to care for. Sonny and Rita were in the service, Bobby and Franklin were out in the world raising families of their own, and now Joe was off to see what his future would bring. I couldn't fight back the tears when my youngest child hugged and kissed me good-bye. I saw there were tears running down his cheeks, too, and he had the same look in his eyes he'd had those many years before when he and Linny sobbed their vows never to part.

That night the house seemed strangely quiet and empty. Sammy and Potey, Joe's two dogs, went into Joe's room to look for him, but of course he wasn't there. I couldn't eat dinner, and in the silence, Steve Szolnoki, my husband, looked at me across the table and said in Hungarian, "How far to Alabama?"

FOUR

Make no mistake about it, my son Joe was a big hit from the very first moment he stepped on the Alabama campus. He and Coach Schnellenberger had no sooner driven into Tuscaloosa when Joe, all dressed up in his nice, new, sporty clothes from Beaver Falls, went over to the practice field and saw the tower that Coach Bryant had built for himself so he could have a bird's-eye view of everything that was going on. Unknown to the other players, Coach Bryant invited Joe up on his tower. He stuck out his hand and said, "Hi, coach. I'm Joe Namath." The rest of that conversation is between Joe and Coach Bryant and God, but on the practice field everybody stopped dead in their tracks and just stared. Nobody in the history of the world had ever been up on that tower except Bear Bryant, not the president of the university, not an assistant coach, and for sure not a player. I think all the other players figured Coach Bryant might take Joe and throw him off the side or something, but they knew right away that Joe was going to be special.

And he was. Here I go with some more football talk, but what happened that first fall might give you a pretty good idea of the kind of football mind Joe had even as a freshman. Joe wasn't brought in with any promises that he was going to be treated like the savior of the Alabama football program. Coach Bryant doesn't work that way, and besides, the year before, the Crimson Tide—that's the Alabama nickname—had lost only one game all year, and in 1961, the year of Joe's arrival, they would win the national championship with a perfect 11–0 record that included a victory over Arkansas in the Sugar Bowl. But within two days Joe was running the sophisticated Alabama offense for the freshman team better than anyone else ever had. That's not just a mother talking, either. A lot of Joe's freshman teammates said the same thing. In Joe's very first scrimmage, when the freshman and the red shirts (upperclassmen who are held out to give them an extra year of varsity eligibility) were supposed to be cannon fodder for that big, powerful varsity, Joe was already checking off plays at the line of scrimmage like he had been born with the Alabama offense in his head.

He was so confident he even kept that toothpick dangling from his mouth until one day right in the middle of a play he suddenly shouted, "Hold it. Time out. Time out, " and got down on his hands and knees and started crawling around on the ground. Everybody thought he had hurt himself, but all he was doing was looking for that toothpick. Right about then the coaches convinced him it might not be too pleasant if somebody's forearm jammed that toothpick down his throat in the middle of a pileup.

There were other examples of his confidence and leadership, too. In one of Alabama's freshman games that fall, against Mississippi State, Joe found himself in a punting situation. It was fourth down and three and Alabama was deep in its own territory clinging to a six-point lead. A center by the name of Gaylon McCollough, who later become a good friend of Joe's, came in from the sidelines specifically to snap the ball for a punt. But in the huddle Joe called a pass play.

"I thought Joe had lost his mind," said Gaylon, "but he calmly told us we had to make that first down to keep State from getting the ball back, and sure enough, he threw a little look-in pass that was right on the money. We eventually did have to punt, but that pass won the game for us because when the gun went off, State was on our four-yard line. Those couple of minutes Joe gained for us by getting the first down made the difference."

The Alabama freshmen team only played three games, but the last one was against the Crimson Tide's deadly intrastate rival, Auburn. Alabama took the opening kickoff and not two minutes had gone by when Joe threw a forty-six-yard touchdown pass to a little end named Creed Gilmer. However, a big, fast Auburn tailback named Tucker Frederickson—the same guy who'd been a high school all-American with Joe—took the following kickoff on his four, ripped up the middle, broke to his left sideline, and didn't stop until he reached the Alabama end zone. With the extra points, that made the score 7–7, and a terrible rainstorm prevented anybody else from moving the ball much for the rest of the afternoon. I only mention this now because for the next three years Joe Namath and Tucker Frederickson were the two biggest football names in the state of Alabama, in the South, and maybe even in the entire country. Their ongoing rivalry played a big part in Joe's life, especially when he turned professional after the 1964 season was over.

I didn't find out right away that Joe's freshman year at Alabama wasn't all good. All of my children, in fact, were reluctant to relay any bad news because they didn't want to hurt me. If something was going wrong in their lives, I might find out second hand—from a school principal, a neighbor, or a friend—but hardly ever from them personally. Still, a mother sometimes gets a sixth sense about such matters. Joe called home a lot, and although it took some time, I eventually found out what his problems were.

What it boiled down to was that Joe was a northern boy at a southern school. About eighty percent of Joe's freshman teammates had been recruited from schools in Alabama, Georgia, and Tennessee, and right in the middle of them was this big, swarthy northerner from someplace called Beaver Falls, Pennsylvania. Today, Joe's got a southern drawl just as honeycovered as the rest of them, but back then he talked differently; he was an outsider, and he just didn't understand, or accept, the attitude white southerners had toward blacks in the early 1960s. The segregation-integration issue was very big at Alabama then, but my gosh, Joe had grown up in a black neighborhood, played with blacks all through his childhood, and until he was twelve years old his closest friend had been black. I don't think Joe knew what racial prejudice was until one day, when he was about ten years old, he and Linny Alford

48 went into a Beaver Falls pizza parlor and heard a waitress say, "We don't want your kind in here."

Joe and Linny were stunned. They didn't know whether it was Linny being black or Joe being honky that offended the lady, and so they both walked out.

Joe said that during his first year at Alabama he was called names like "Yankee Traitor," "Nigger Lover," and "Redneck," and that he just didn't know what to make of it all. Why, he even started calling himself "Joe Willie" so he could have a double first name like "Bobby Joe" or "Lee Roy" or a lot of the other good ole boys. But it didn't work. Joe spoke up when he was asked about racial matters, and his opinions generated a lot of hostility.

I had always assumed Joe would be judged by his ability as a football player and by his honesty at Alabama, but apparently some of his teammates thought he was a Union boy in blue come down to free the South. It finally came to the point that in one telephone conversation, his voice quavering, Joe said, "I'm going to quit."

Well, when he said that, I put Franklin, who just happened to be standing by, on the phone.

"What's this bull about you quitting?" he asked. (That Franklin always did have a way with words.) "I'll tell you this just once. Name-calling doesn't hurt anywhere near as much as the whipping you'll get if you come back here a quitter."

Joe had something up his sleeve. He knew if he ever did leave Alabama he could walk right out and sign a major league baseball contract, and for big money, too. In his senior year in high school Joe batted something like .385 for a team that went 18–0 and won the western Pennsylvania interscholastic championship. He was a good pitcher, too, but preferred to play left field because he didn't want to hurt his throwing arm for football. That summer he played with an American Legion team, the Colonel Joseph H. Thompson Post 261 "Tommies," who amassed a 26–4 record. Joe was serious about his baseball, too. Although he was named to the prestigious Big 33 Pennsylvania high school all-stars, who played a national all-star team every summer in Hershey, Joe turned down the honor because the Tommies were involved in district and regional playoffs. Later that summer he attended a big tryout camp at Monessen, where scouts from all twenty-six major league teams were on hand. According to Dom Casey, his American Legion coach, the "book" on Joe was that he had a tremendous throwing arm and always gave 100 percent, and you couldn't get a fastball by him, although he did have some trouble hitting a curve.

Most of the baseball clubs backed off when they learned Joe was trying to go to college on a football scholarship, but the Baltimore Orioles did offer him $20,000 to sign. That seemed like a fortune to me, but just as I had done with Franklin a few years earlier, I sat Joe down in the kitchen and made it perfectly clear that college came first.

Still, when he left for Alabama, he told Casey, "I love baseball; if any club gets up to $30,000, give me a call."

Joe was ready, and so were the Chicago Cubs, who now dangled a $50,000 bonus contract in his face. The Alabama coaches must have found out about it because they immediately got hold of a former major league pitcher named Emery "Bubba" Church to tell Joe the facts of life.

"Look, Joe, they'll give you a $50,000 bonus, and you'll blow that in two years," Church said. "You know you will. Then suppose your arm goes bad. Every pitcher knows that can happen—just like that. Then what have you got? No college degree, nothing."*

I don't know whether it was Church's influence, or Franklin's, or maybe even mine, but of course Joe decided to stick it out at Alabama. He began to make some new friends around Tuscaloosa, and in general things just started getting better and better for him. I couldn't have been happier. (Just as an aside, it's also interesting to note that if you watch Alabama on television these days, you'll see just about as many blacks playing for the Crimson Tide as there are playing for northern schools like Penn State, Michigan, and Ohio State. I think that's a sign of real progress.)

When Joe came home from school after that up-and-down freshman year, I could tell he had made the adjustment to Alabama—or maybe it was that Alabama had made an adjustment to him. I was never sure which. He threw a football around to keep in shape, but he also talked a lot about the charm and beauty of the Deep South. Pretty soon, I knew I'd have to go and see the place for myself, and there didn't seem

---

*Namath. (New York: Rostam Publishing, Inc., 1969), p. 25.

to be a better time than to watch Joe make his debut as the quarterback of the Alabama varsity on September 22, 1962.

If you think Joe's sudden departure had been traumatic the year before, you should have seen the way everybody carried on about mine. I guess I wasn't exactly what you'd call a world traveler, although I had made that sixty-five mile trip to Massillon, Ohio, several times, and had run down to Pittsburgh on occasion.

At the airport, everybody bustled around in a mass of confusion. Franklin was the worst of all. He acted like a little old lady as he checked the schedule and my tickets, then rechecked everything and finally re-rechecked them again. At last I got on board, and as the plane started down the runway I started to pray. I had never flown before, and although I wasn't particularly nervous, I did want to make sure everything turned out for the best. A little prayer never hurts in those circumstances.

Several prayers later, my ears started to pop as we came in for a landing. In a jiffy I was inside the terminal looking around for Joe.

He was no place to be seen, and no wonder. I finally saw a big sign that informed me I had disembarked in Atlanta. After several conversations with unamused airline personnel, I was again on my way to Alabama—six hours late—to find out what kind of life my youngest son was leading.

Tuscaloosa, I am happy to report, is a charming southern university town. But it did take me awhile to get used to certain southern customs. The first people I stayed with were Mr. and Mrs. Riggs Stephenson. He was a prominent Alabama alumnus who had been an all-conference fullback for the Crimson Tide back in 1923 and later picked up the nickname "Iron Legs" during a short major league baseball career with the Pittsburgh Pirates. Riggs and his wife—I always called her "Miz Riggs" just like her southern friends did—were perfect hosts, but I'll never forget my first day with them. Miz Riggs kept talking about getting up early in the morning, which was fine with me because in Beaver Falls I got up pretty early myself. But when the household turned in around eight o'clock, I wondered just exactly what they meant by "early."

I had my own room and I turned on the television. Eight o'clock was a little early, even by my standards. Finally, a little past midnight I fell asleep, and it didn't seem but a few minutes later when I was awakened by the sounds of the house coming to life. I looked at my clock. It was five o'clock. I said, "Rose, honey, this is ridiculous."

Then I heard a gentle rapping on the door as Miz Riggs said, "Rose? C'mon now. We let you sleep an extra half hour."

It didn't take me long to figure out why the Stephensons got up so early. By midday the weather was so hot and muggy, it was obvious the only time to get anything accomplished was first thing in the morning. Even in September.

There were other people I wanted to meet, too. During his freshman year, Joe had talked about three sisters, all middle-aged widows, who had befriended him and other members of the football team. Their names were Bessie Asbury, Ruth Burchfield, and Mary Kraut, and when I got to know them, they became close friends of mine as well. They were just three wonderful people who felt sorry for the boys who had come to school so far away from home and did everything they could to make them welcome in Tuscaloosa. They practically kept an open house. They'd always have pork chops, corn bread, and all those other southern goodies spread out in a continual feast for those kids. For some reason they had taken a special liking to Joe—I think it was because he was the farthest from home of any of the players—and later, when Joe took an off-campus apartment, they were constantly sneaking over on little recon-naissance missions. No coffeepot? Next day Joe would have a coffeepot. No radio? Next day there'd be a radio. Or a little television. Or even a roasting pan with knives and forks. They were three fine southern ladies, and Joe and I remain close to them even to this day.

It was Miz Riggs, though, who introduced me to the person I most wanted to meet—Paul "Bear" Bryant. I'd heard so much about him that I just had to see the man for myself. One night it was arranged, and just the two of us, Miz Riggs and myself, went over to the Bryants' house. I really didn't know what to expect, but when he and his wife, Mary Harmon, came to the door, I realized right away that Coach Bryant is even bigger in person than he looks in his pictures. I understood how he could have wrestled and beaten that bear, just like he said he did.

He certainly had a forceful personality, but after I got over my nervousness, I saw a little twinkle in his eye and I suspected that deep down inside he was really just a teddy bear. I'd never want to cross him, though. I've been told by a very reliable source—Joe—that the best policy with Coach Bryant is to do what he tells you and don't ask questions, at least on the football field.

Coach Bryant and Mary Harmon couldn't have been nicer. Mary Harmon said those stories about the Bear buying his suits two sizes too large really were true. "He used to get so nervous on the sidelines he'd just rip and tear his suits apart," she said. I didn't have any trouble believing her.

Coach Bryant took me downstairs to his trophy room and it was fantastic. Trophies, silver bowls, footballs, and I don't know what all else were down there, a very impressive collection for his very memorable career.

Coach Bryant and I were making small talk when I told him, "Now you make sure Joe behaves. If he does something wrong, you be sure and correct him."

And I remember Coach Bryant just threw back his head and roared. It was a jolly laugh, the way a jolly bear ought to laugh.

Coach Bryant and Joe got along superbly. They couldn't have been called close friends when Joe was in school, because that's not the relationship between a coach and his players, but each had a great admiration for the other right from the beginning.

Coach Bryant made it a point to be close to all his quarterbacks. He felt they were extensions of himself out there on the field, and he spent long hours walking and talking with them to find out what kind of people they really were. It was something he had to know in order to be a good coach. But I always liked to think Joe's relationship with Coach Bryant was something special. I think Coach Bryant often went out of his way for Joe. He knew my son was a long way from home and he understood the problems Joe had, especially that first year. Of course, Coach Bryant knew that Joe came from a broken home. I'm no psychologist, but maybe Coach Bryant became something of a father figure for Joe, even more than a coach normally is for his players.

In the end, though, I think it just came down to the fact that Coach Bryant is 100 percent a man, from his good-luck hat and his oversized suits down to his growlish, bearlike voice. What else could you do except admire him? That goes not only for Joe and me, but for anybody.

Finally, the three sisters and I made the short drive over to Legion Field in Birmingham, where Alabama would face Georgia in the first game of the year—and Joe's first game as a collegian. The most people I had ever seen in one place were the 10,000 or 12,000 who came to watch Beaver Falls High School play at Reeves Stadium, and I wasn't really prepared for the 53,000 folks who jammed the stadium that Saturday night to see the Crimson Tide begin its defense of the national championship. The four of us—Bessie, Ruth, Mary, and I—made great cheerleaders. Even though our seats were high in the stands, I'll bet the players heard us all the way down on the field.

Alabama took the opening kickoff, but on its first series of downs nothing much happened. I started to wonder if something might be wrong. On the very next series of plays, however, Joe dropped back to throw, and on exactly the fourth play of his varsity career hurled a fifty-two-yard touchdown pass to Richard Williamson. That was more like it. From then on it was all Alabama. Joe completed ten of fourteen passes for 179 yards and two touchdowns as Alabama won easily, 35–0. I couldn't have been prouder, especially since Joe had replaced an all-American quarterback named Pat Trammel, and I knew a lot was expected of him. I was even prouder the next day when I saw the newspapers were already predicting great things for my son.

That Georgia-Alabama game was important to me, of course, because it was the first time I had seen Joe play college ball. And the following March the game took on added significance when *The Saturday Evening Post* charged that Coach Bryant and Wally Butts, the Georgia athletic director and former head coach, had contrived to "fix" the contest. When I heard the story, I knew right away it couldn't be true; Coach Bryant just wasn't the kind of man who'd even consider something like that. A few years later the courts agreed. Wally Butts was awarded an in-court judgment of $460,000 for the libel, and Coach Bryant settled out of court for $300,000. That's a lot of money, but I don't believe any amount of cash could have adequately compensated the two men for all the agony the suit put them through.

I had planned originally to stay in Alabama for only a week, but I was having such a good time I extended my vacation through another football weekend—and gained a few more insights into the kind of life my Joe was leading. On one occasion Joe introduced me to Jack Warner, the president of the Gulf States Paper Company, who everybody called "Ole Jack." I practically expected him to be grey haired and senile, but he turned out to be tall, athletic, and handsome, and he wore just about the nicest smile in the whole world.

I was even awed by his company's office building. Paintings from all over the world hung on the walls, carpets from the Middle East covered the floors, and right in the middle of the lobby was this absolutely fabulous garden. The place looked more like a vacation spa than an office building.

Ole Jack, it turned out, was a good friend to Alabama football. During the off-season he gave some of the players odd jobs around his mill. He understood that college is a rough road and sometimes a little extra spending money comes in handy.

"Besides," Mr. Warner told me, "putting the boys in the mill keeps them off the street and out of trouble, and when there's something to do, the boys will make a good job of it."

I thought about his new job for a while, but then I was off again, this time to meet Art Catrino, another friend of Joe's who owned a restaurant called Art's Char House right across the street from the practice field. Joe took me into the back room and showed me his favorite table. And right in the corner of Joe's favorite table was carved: "The Pennsylvania Kid Was Here, JWN."

"Don't worry, Rose," Art said. "That table only cost me $75. The way Joe's going, it'll be worth twice that when he's through here."

"Besides," said Art, "it's cheaper to have Joe out here carving his initials than it is to have him in the kitchen. He comes in here and says, 'Art, I'm Italian.' Has anybody ever seen an Hungarian-Italian? 'And back home in Beaver Falls I make the world's greatest pizzas.' I shoulda known better than to challenge him on it," said Art. "He's back of the counter before I know what's happenin' buildin' the five biggest, most expensive pizzas, puttin' everything in the place on 'em. If that wasn't bad enough, he has the Alabama football team waiting outside to taste 'em. On top of that, with those giant hands of his, he palms three doughnuts right out from under me. Rose, when he makes all-American, remember it's my doughnuts that did it."

I was beginning to understand that in some ways Joe hadn't changed one bit since he left Beaver Falls. Not one bit at all.

Finally, my little visit came to an end, and I went back to Beaver Falls—I even got off the plane at the right airport—and spent the rest of the 1962 season watching the Crimson Tide on television or hanging on the radio Saturday nights trying to find its scores. In many ways the long wait was more nerve-racking than being there in person. I'm a very devout Catholic, and I made it a point to say a special prayer by the statue of Saint Mary before every game. Mainly I prayed for the safety of all the ballplayers on both sides, but I also did kind of hint that another Tide victory sure would be appreciated. "So please, Holy Mary," I said, "keep all the boys from serious injury—and maybe let Alabama score a few more points than its opponents." It didn't always work, of course, but I felt a little better knowing the Blessed Mother was watching over a good Catholic quarterback playing against all those Southern Baptists.

Joe's sophomore year went by fast. Alabama won and won; after eight games its record was 8–0 and the Tide was ranked the No. 1 team in the country by a big margin. Then Joe and his teammates went to Atlanta to play Georgia Tech. In their game the year before, an Alabama player named Darwin Holt had blocked a Georgia Tech player named Chick Graning, and in a fluke accident Holt's forearm got up inside Graning's helmet and fractured his jaw. It was one chance in a thousand and no penalty was called on the play, but the Atlanta papers jumped all over Coach Bryant and charged him with teaching dirty football. In my opinion the papers were totally unfair. Coach Bryant's teams have always played hard, never dirty. But by the time the two teams met again, the incident had turned the rivalry into a vicious feud. Tech played way over its head and late in the fourth quarter they led, 7–6. Then Joe went to work and brought Alabama down to the Tech fourteen-yard line, first and ten. At the very least it looked like Alabama could kick an easy field goal to win, but Coach Bryant took Joe out of the game and let another quarterback, Jack Hurlbut, throw a pass. It was intercepted and Tech hung on for the win.

The loss cost Alabama a second straight national championship, and even to this day, it's a game Joe can't forget. Like all winners, he doesn't remember the games he's won nearly as much as the games he's lost. But he took the defeat like a true sportsman and in the last game of the season, against Auburn, he did something that really showed his colors.

Alabama was winning easily that afternoon, something like 38–0, and Joe hadn't played much at all in the fourth quarter. But with two minutes to go, an assistant coach phoned down from the press box to Coach Bryant that Joe needed just thirty yards to set an all-time Alabama season record for total offense. Coach Bryant hurriedly sent Joe back into action, but on his first play he lost seven yards. Nevertheless, a long pass would have given him the record. Instead, Joe called for a quick kick from his own twenty-eight-yard line. All Joe said was, "I didn't want to have a mistake happen that would have allowed Auburn to score. We wanted a shutout."

I was proud of my boy that afternoon, but I wasn't surprised. Joe never was one for personal glory. His team always came first, whether it was Beaver Falls High School, the University of Alabama, or later, the New York Jets.

New Year's Eve has always been a crazy time around my house. The whole family comes over and with hordes of grandchildren running around—I have eighteen right now, plus a great-grandchild—our celebrations get pretty hectic. New Year's Eve of 1962 was especially significant. The next day Joe would be playing in the Orange Bowl against Oklahoma, and of course the entire clan would be watching on television. We were having just a grand old time bringing in the new year when suddenly I heard something shatter in the living room. Franklin's oldest son, Michael, had crashed into my statue of Saint Mary and had simply shattered it. I was shattered, too. I knew I'd need that statue the next day—to pray for the players' safety, of course.

That night and all the next morning I tried different ways to pray. I used a scapular. I tried the Rosary both in English and in Hungarian. I even prayed before the crucifix, but it just wasn't the same. The Blessed Mother is my favorite saint, and I knew that somewhere out there in America somebody was talking with the dear Mother on Oklahoma's behalf. Besides, I knew President Kennedy, another good Catholic, was a close friend of Bud Wilkinson, the Oklahoma coach, and would be at the game sitting on the Sooners' side.

As the game time drew near, Franklin and little Mike went out and tried to find a new statue. No luck. All the stores were closed. I was worried and had just about given up hope when I saw Franklin's car pull in the driveway—with a statue of Saint Mary standing beside him in the front seat. It turned out Franklin and Mike had coaxed the good father of a nearby church into letting me borrow Saint Mary for the afternoon.

"Okay, Oklahoma," I shouted. "Just you wait." I knew nobody would be praying to Her and watching the game at the same time, not even the President. The power of prayer is wonderful to behold. Nobody got hurt and the final score that afternoon was Alabama 17, Oklahoma 0.

Joe's junior year at Alabama, the season of 1963, was more of the same—almost. The Tide won their first three games easily but in the fourth they were upset by Florida, 10–6. After four more wins it looked like they were back on the right track, but on a windy afternoon in late November they were upset by Auburn, 10–8, with that fellow Tucker Frederickson doing most of the damage. Two losses in one year! Why, by Alabama standards it was a disaster, but it didn't begin to compare with what happened a week later.

On a Sunday morning, the week after the Auburn game, I received a telephone call from Coach Bryant, and I knew immediately something was terribly wrong.

"Rose, I wanted to tell you before you heard it on radio and television," he said in that deep voice of his, "but I had to suspend Joe from the team for breaking one of our rules."

His voice seemed very sad. He explained that a friend of his had told him he'd seen Joe drunk and directing traffic in downtown Tuscaloosa the day before. "Now, Rose," Coach Bryant went on, "the person that came to me is a man I trust and respect, but I believe in Joe, too. He's never lied to me about anything, and he said he was watching the Army-Navy game on television. I believe that, but he did admit to taking a sip from a drink later that night at a fraternity party. Our rules are strict about that kind of thing and they apply to everybody. If I let Joe off, it wouldn't be fair to him or his teammates or to the things I believe in. I have to suspend him. I don't want to, but I have to."

What really happened only Joe knows. He's never told me, and there are at least three versions of the incident. The first was what Coach Bryant's friend told him, the second was what

Joe told Coach Bryant, and the third was that he'd had a couple of beers before going to the opening game of the Alabama basketball season that night.

Whatever happened, I feel now that rules are rules and Coach Bryant was right in what he did. It made Joe a better man. But I sure didn't see it that way at first. I cried and pleaded with Coach Bryant not to punish Joe. Coach Bryant was very calm, and as we talked I even came around to his point of view. In fact, by the time we hung up I was all for it. I even felt like administering a little discipline myself.

The rest of that Sunday I couldn't help thinking about how calm and relaxed Coach Bryant sounded. I even started to wonder whether he'd really go through with it. After all, it couldn't be a very easy thing for him to suspend a player who was maybe the best quarterback in the country.

Then I received another call, this one from Art Catrino, the owner of the restaurant, Art's Char House, where Joe had carved that inscription in the table. From the way Art was whispering, I thought I was getting a call from a spy or something. He said to keep it quiet, but everything was okay. He was going to take care of Joe until he earned his way back on the team.

Was Coach Bryant really mad then?

Now, I knew Coach Bryant couldn't walk on water any more than Joe could feed the Beaver Falls football team with fishes and loaves, but I had heard the story of how he'd made the rain stop. Just before game time one Saturday afternoon it was coming down buckets, but when the Bear led his team out on the field, it stopped. Just like that. And the sun began shining.

Art pretty much convinced me Joe wasn't going to have an easy time of it, and he didn't. Fortunately for his teammates, the second-string quarterback was a fine, upstanding fellow named Steve Sloan, and he led the Crimson Tide to a victory over Miami of Florida in the last game of the season as well to a 12–7 upset of Ole Miss in the Sugar Bowl.

Joe walked a fine line the next few months. He never called home because I think he knew what my reaction would be, but when spring practice rolled around he was chompin' at the bit. In the first intrasquad scrimmage, played before 14,000 fans in Tuscaloosa's Denny Stadium—that's more people than ever saw Joe play in Beaver Falls—he threw a fifty-two-yard touchdown pass to Ray Perkins on the second play of the game and during one stretch completed seven straight.

Joe wasn't afraid to call home any more. He phoned to tell me he'd won his old job back and couldn't wait for the 1964 season to begin.

Neither could I, and like I had two seasons before, I made the trip south for the Georgia opener. From high in the stands it did me proud to watch my son warm up along the sidelines. He was fast becoming a legend in the South, and Alabama was again picked to be a strong contender for the national championship.

During the pregame festivities, a man sitting in the row behind me kept shouting, "C'mon, nose, c'mon."

I didn't think that sounded particularly nice, but I wasn't about to say anything. I just wanted to sit back and enjoy the game.

But when the game started, the name-calling continued: "C'mon, nose. Let's go, nose."

Still I kept quiet.

Then it happened. "C'mon, Namath. C'mon, nose. Move that Tide."

Well, I was incensed. I must admit Joe does have a prominent nose, but I still didn't like this guy to be calling my son names. I turned around—and found myself looking into the biggest nose I'd ever seen in my life. It looked like Pinocchio's or even Cyrano de Bergerac's. This guy had nerve.

"Let me introduce myself," I said. "I'm Joe Namath's mother, and after the game I think we ought to measure noses, just to see how much bigger yours really is."

I've never seen anybody so abashed. The man offered profuse apologies, and, in fact, southern charm won out even before the game was over. We spent the rest of the game chatting with each other and cheering on the Tide to another victory.

After the Georgia game I did some more sightseeing around the campus for a very specific reason. Joe sometimes complained about the strict training rules Coach Bryant had, and he also said he didn't like being shut up in the athletic dorm all during the football season. The way he described it, the place was almost like a prison. Naturally, I had to see for myself. Well, in 1963 the university built a little place for the athletes called Paul W. Bryant Hall—it took a special act of the Alabama state legislature to name the building for a living person—and when I saw it you could have knocked me over with a feather. It didn't look like a dormitory at all, much less a prison. It looked like something out of *Gone With the Wind.* It had a beautiful columned façade, a magnificent circular lobby, and each of the rooms had deep, lush carpets, and private bath. And the training table food! My gosh, there was sometimes more food for one meal than we got to eat in an entire week back during the good old days in Beaver Falls. I didn't feel quite so concerned about Joe's "prison" digs after taking a look at all that.

Following the win over Georgia, Alabama scored victories over Tulane and Vanderbilt and looked better every week. But in the fourth game of the year, against North Carolina State, Joe suffered a setback of far-reaching significance.

The game started routinely enough. Joe completed the first seven of eight passes he threw and midway through the second period, although neither side had scored, it was clear the Tide was in the driver's seat. Then it happened. Joe took the snap from center and sprinted out to his right, planted his right foot, and cut back left—and just collapsed. This time, as he writhed on the ground, he wasn't doing anything as frivolous as looking for a toothpick. His right knee had given out and he was badly hurt. To this day, nobody knows for sure what happened.

Joe assured me over the telephone that the Alabama doctors didn't feel the injury was permanent, but I started to think about something that had happened in his childhood. When Joe was seven, his father took him to Doylestown, Pennsylvania, on a little outing and he came down with a terrible fever. His legs hurt so badly we all feared he had polio. We took him to several doctors, but none of them could find anything wrong. Eventually the fever went away and the pain stopped, but I always wondered whether his legs might have been somehow weakened then. Except for the normal bumps and bruises any football player gets, however, Joe had absolutely no problems with his legs until that game against North Carolina State.

At Alabama, Joe always taped his shoes for added support— that's how his white shoes thing got started, not out of any desire to be a hot dog—and it's a strange coincidence that against N.C. State Joe neglected to use the tape for the first and only time that season.

The real reason for his injury, though, was the simple fact that Joe was a superb athlete. He was only six feet one inch, but he could dunk a basketball backwards, for example, something a lot of much taller basketball players can't even do. He was a natural at almost everything he tried, from football and baseball to golf and snooker.

Coach Bryant realized this as soon as Joe joined his team. Until then Coach Bryant had pretty much turned out defense-minded clubs, like most southern schools, but once he saw Joe's potential, he immediately put in a special sprint-out offense. Most quarterbacks operate from what is called a pro set, in which they are only required to hand the ball off to somebody, to drop back three or four steps, and to throw. A sprint-out quarterback, however, is required to take several quick steps to the left or right on every play, then decide whether he's going to pass or run. People tend to forget that Joe was an excellent running quarterback until he got hurt, and it was on one of these sprint-outs that he first injured himself.

I'm occasionally asked why Joe didn't have his knee operated on right away. As I understand it, in an injury like Joe's, fluid builds up around the knee to protect it from further damage. If, when the knee is drained, the fluid is clear, it's a sign there's no serious damage. If the fluid is bloody, it usually means an operation. Joe's knees were drained frequently, a very painful process that involved a big needle about four inches long, and I get sick just thinking about it. There was no blood, and everybody thought Joe would be okay before very long.

He wasn't. He only played off and on the rest of the year, but whenever he did get into a game, he made his presence felt. Joe didn't start that year against Georgia Tech. This was to be the last game of a long rivalry, and the bitterness from two and three years before still hadn't quieted down. Coach Bryant, in fact, walked onto the field in Atlanta wearing a football helmet, just in case a few of the Tech partisans decided to let fly with a whiskey bottle or something. As they had in the famous 1962 upset, those Ramblin' Recks were playing over their heads and with ninety seconds left in the first half the score was 0–0.

Enter Joe Namath, bad leg and all. Now, I should explain right here that several players have told me Joe ran a good huddle. Nobody ever said a word to him. His teammates knew he was always thinking two or three plays ahead and wouldn't have dreamed of interfering with his concentration.

All the players were down on one knee getting sips of water when Joe came in. Joe said, "Okay. I've been watching these guys and I think we can score right away if everybody will carry out their assignments."

Two plays later Joe completed a pass to David Ray, now a kicker for the Los Angeles Rams, and Alabama was on the one. Steve Bowman carried the ball in and Alabama had six, just like that.

Joe and the Tide weren't through, however. Alabama tried an onside kick, recovered it, and again Joe limped into the huddle and told the players how they were going to score a second time. By now they were true believers, and sure enough, the score at half time was Alabama 14, Georgia Tech 0.

With Joe and Steve Sloan alternating at quarterback, Alabama finished up an undefeated season with a hard-fought victory over that pesky Auburn bunch, 21–14. This was despite another great performance by Tucker Frederickson, who played fifty-eight minutes, ran for 117 yards in twenty-two carries, and scored one touchdown. The win earned them the national championship, which was voted on before the bowl games that year. Then it came time to go back to the Orange Bowl in Miami and play the champions of the Southwest Conference, the University of Texas.

Joe invited me down to Miami and I was more than ready to go. Right away I found out that Joe had been talking to some people about signing a professional contract. He was so confident he even told me I could buy myself anything I wanted. I was a little leery. I could still remember those lean years of the Depression and all that rabbit and homemade soup. But Joe insisted, and so I went out and did things up in fine style. I must have charged $100 worth of little goodies on my spree.

Several days before the game, though, Joe reinjured his right knee. He was listed as a doubtful starter and I suddenly got worried about two things: Joe's knee and my spending spree. Joe said he had arrived at a "complete understanding" with the New York Jets, although no contract could be signed until after the Orange Bowl. But I knew gentlemen's agreements sometimes didn't hold up, and now, with his leg hurt again, his future could be in shambles.

Joe was unconcerned. "Don't worry," he said. "The Jets had a specialist look at my leg and he said it would be 100 percent after an operation. I'm still signing with them."

I wasn't totally convinced until I met Sonny Werblin, the part-owner and president of the Jets. Werblin invited me to sit with him during the game, and it didn't take more than a couple of minutes to know his handshake was as good as a written contract.

Not only was Joe a doubtful starter, he didn't play at all during the first quarter. Right away Texas jumped off to a 14–0 lead. Ernie Koy ran seventy-nine yards for the Longhorn's first touchdown, and Jim Hudson threw a sixty-nine-yard pass to George Sauer for their second.

Joe hobbled on the field for the first time early in the second quarter, and right away Alabama began to move. Joe completed six passes for eighty-one yards and suddenly the score was 14–7. I felt a little better, but Texas came back to score a third touchdown and at half time the Longhorns led, 21–7.

The second half of that game was probably the most exciting thirty minutes of football I've ever seen. In the third quarter, Alabama made some adjustments in their offensive game plan designed to loosen up the Texas defense, and Joe, bad knee and all, hit Ray Perkins for a touchdown pass to narrow the Texas lead to 21–14. When David Ray kicked a field goal near the end of the third quarter to bring Alabama within four, 21–17, I was almost sure Joe would leave Alabama a winner.

During that last frantic quarter of play, as Joe tried desperately to get that go-ahead touchdown, Mr. Werblin kept jumping up and down and saying, "Namath, you're terrific. I'm not paying you enough."

I tapped Mr. Werblin on the arm and said, "If that's the way you feel about it, why not pay him more?"

What did I know?

Texas put up a good fight, but Joe kept plugging away, and with less than two minutes to go, Alabama had the ball first and goal on the Alabama six-yard line. Everybody in the whole Orange Bowl was just going wild and I suspect everybody watching on television was, too.

Three times Joe handed off to his running backs, and three times the Texas defense, led by middle linebacker Tommy Nobis, bent but didn't break. Now it was fourth down and one foot to go, and the roars from the stands were just deafening.

Joe called a quarterback sneak. He found a tiny, tiny hole and followed it into the end zone. Touchdown, Alabama!

At least that's what I thought at first, because one of the

officials ran into the huge pileup at the goal line, took the ball away from Joe, and signaled a touchdown. Then another official came over to the first official and began discussing the situation. Then a third official came over and didn't discuss anything with anybody. He just put the ball back down on the six-inch line and gave it over to Texas.

I couldn't believe what I was seeing, but once those guys in the striped shirts make a decision, that's it.

And that's the way the most exciting college football game ever played ended: Texas 21, Alabama 17.

I felt terrible for Joe and his teammates, even though he did get the most valuable player award, but the next morning he was all smiles and bouncing around in unbelievably good spirits.

I didn't understand, but at a press conference later that day it all became clear.

My son the quarterback had signed a contract to play football with the New York Jets for $427,000.

That press conference was icing on the cake to the most exciting two weeks of my life. Everybody was there—Coach Bryant, of course, Weeb Ewbank, the roly-poly coach of the Jets, Sonny Werblin, and even George Wallace, the governor of Alabama. I took the opportunity to thank Governor Wallace for a nice telegram he'd sent to Joe and his teammates before the Orange Bowl and had a pleasant time just making small talk with him.

Then Joe and Mr. Werblin took the podium, and with all those television lights blazing and cameras whirring, Mr. Werblin made the announcement that Joe had signed with the Jets. Nobody said anything about money right then, but the news broadcasts that night said the figure was $427,000, and I got light-headed and almost giddy every time I heard it. This is how Joe's first contract was divided up: $225,000 as a bonus to be spread out over several years; $25,000 in salary for each of the next three years; $30,000 for lawyers' fees; and the rest of it went in salaries for the next three years for Joe's two brothers, Bobby and Franklin, and his sister Rita's husband, all of whom were made members of the Jets' scouting staff. It was generous of Joe to include his family in his good fortune. He certainly wasn't asked to do it, and I've always thought highly of his kindness.

The final touch was a $7,000 green Lincoln Continental. That was a nice gesture on Mr. Werblin's part. I guess if you're paying somebody $400,000 or so, another seven grand is just small change, but to Joe it meant a lot more. The Lincoln was the first real automobile he'd ever owned. Oh, when he was a sophomore at Alabama, he and the team manager, a young man named Jack "Hoot Owl" Hicks, had gone halves on an old 1952 four-door Ford. It cost them all of $25 apiece, and when I saw it I could understand why. That four-door didn't have *any* doors. None at all. And it must have had a top speed of about twenty-five miles an hour. A real classic.

With all the Orange Bowl and contract hoopla out of the way, Joe and my husband and I decided to take a little vacation in Miami Beach. Steve and Joe spent most of the time fishing together while I sat on the beach basking in the sun.

Then we drove back to Tuscaloosa. For the first time in his life, Joe had a little spending money—actually, a lot of it—and he made the most of a good situation. Everywhere we stopped he'd walk into some gas station or restaurant and flash a big wad of bills. I don't know for sure how much he had with him. It was probably around a thousand dollars, but to me it looked like a million.

"Be careful, Joe," I kept insisting. "You want somebody to hit you over the head? Don't be showing off all that money."

It wasn't any use. Joe was a very trusting person. "Nobody's gonna steal my money," he said. "Don't be worrying."

I tried not to, but I don't mind telling you I was much relieved when we made it safely back to Tuscaloosa.

The first stop was Art's Char House. When Joe had been suspended the year before, Art Catrino had let Joe run a tab, and I was proud to see the first thing Joe was doing now that he had some money was paying off his debts. Even in the worst years, it was important to us that our family always pay off debts.

Art's eyes just went buggy when he saw Joe come in flashing his roll.

"What in hell are you doing with all that?" Art demanded.

"Paying you back."

"I appreciate it sure enough, but you don't owe me no $18,000 or whatever it is you've got there. You know? Here you are going through college and getting dumber all the time. Carrying all that money around is just gonna give somebody the idea to smack your head open. I thought you'd be smarter than that."

Joe got pretty sheepish. "Damn if you aren't right, Art."

"Damn right I'm right."

Joe kept damning and righting and Art kept righting and damning, and pretty soon I wondered whether Joe had heard a word I'd said on our trip. But if I couldn't make Joe listen to sense, I was glad to know he had a friend who could.

A few days later Steve and I flew back to Beaver Falls while Joe went on up to New York City for an operation on his bad knee, and all the time I still couldn't help but wonder at what had happened to my son over the past four years. Just before Joe went to Alabama, Larry Bruno, his high school football coach, had paid him exactly four dollars to haul a load of trash over to the city dump, and now, less than four years later, Sonny Werblin was paying him *$400,000* to play football. Now as I've said, I don't know that much about football, but I do know enough to realize Joe was a good quarterback. All the same, that $400,000 boggled my mind. Was he really worth that much? After all, Joe set very few records at Alabama; he was never a first-team all-American selection in his three years there—in fact, he only made the all-Southeastern Conference first team once, his senior year. And he had a bad knee. Yet Sonny Werblin thought enough of Joe to pay him $400,000. It took me a long time to figure out what was going on.

In 1964, of course, there were two rival football leagues, the old, established National Football League and the new, struggling American Football League. The only way the AFL could get the best college players to play for them was to offer tremendous sums of money in the form of bonus contracts. The NFL had to follow suit, and the bidding war that resulted made a lot of players rich in a hurry. Joe came along at just the right time to take advantage of all this. It really didn't seem to make much difference which team in a particular league signed a particular player; what was important was which *league* signed the prominent collegians, and it was rumored that to help that along all sorts of secret drafts were held and backroom deals made.

Two factors helped to make Joe a member of the Jets. In New York, the most important city in either league because of its size and instant access to the national media, there were two teams—the Jets of the AFL and the Giants of the NFL. In 1963 they had gotten into a much-publicized war over the services of Matt Snell, the big Ohio State fullback. The Jets won Snell and the Giants lost face. So when the 1964 draft rolled around, the Giants, who had the first pick, made sure to draft a player who they knew wanted to play in the NFL. That player, ironically, was Tucker Frederickson, the big Auburn tailback who had given Alabama all it could handle during Joe's four years there. The Giants thought long and hard about drafting Joe themselves. They didn't, fearing to lose him to the Jets and Mr. Sonny Werblin, the second factor in Joe's emergence as a Jet.

Werblin had made a name for himself in show business as a theatrical agent—one of his later clients was Johnny Carson—and he firmly believed in the star system. He felt that if the AFL could get a real star in its biggest, most important city, the league would have it made. And the player he settled on, of course, was my son Joe.

But not right away. In 1964 there were two college quarterbacks who were considered excellent professional prospects, Joe Namath of Alabama and Jerry Rhome of Tulsa. On paper, at least, Rhome had far better records. He set all sorts of NCAA passing records for most touchdowns, most yards gained, and things like that. Werblin knew he was good. Werblin also knew he wasn't a star.

Here's how Werblin explained it to a reporter a few months later:

"I believe in the star system," Sonny said. "It's the only thing that sells tickets. It's what you put on the stage or the playing field that draws people."

"Joe has what we call star quality," Werblin added. "If we knew what makes star quality, it would be easy to reproduce. But you either have it, or you don't. We were still dickering with Namath at the Orange Bowl game when he played for Alabama a few years ago and when he came in to the game that day 72,000 fans moved to the edge of their seats. This is star quality."*

So what Werblin did was dicker with the Houston Oilers, who

Namath (New York: Rostam Publishing, Inc., 1969), p. 30.

had the absolute first pick in the AFL draft, to get the rights to
Joe.

At the same time, the NFL wasn't going to give up Joe without a fight, even if the Giants were. On the first round of the NFL draft, Joe was picked by the St. Louis Cardinals. That set up the battle: the Jets against the Cardinals, the AFL against the NFL, and Joe caught delightfully in the middle.

Meanwhile, down in Tuscaloosa, Joe was trying to get ready for the Orange Bowl and be cool about the pro draft all at the same time. When it became apparent he might, just might, be offered a whole lot of money, he went to Coach Bryant for a little fiscal advice.

Coach Bryant said he told Joe, "Ask 'em for $200,000 and see if they offer $100,000."

Right about then, I think, Joe sensed he might have a pretty good thing going, and right about then, he also decided he might need some help if the bidding really became wild. At Alabama he'd become close friends with a law student named Mike Bite, and from that moment on Mike handled the bulk of the negotiations, which, in fact, did become a lot more than wild.

But Joe never let the bidding war go to his head, not really. As I've mentioned, his center at Alabama was Gaylon McCollough, who had become a pool-playing buddy as well since their freshman days, and in that same NFL draft, Gaylon had been picked by the Dallas Cowboys. "I knew Joe had been contacted by both the Jets and the Cowboys," Gaylon said, "and I wanted to know what kind of figure they were both offering, because I thought the Cowboys' offer to me was unreasonably low. So one night when we were shooting pool, he told me. By then it was up to around $230,000–$240,000 and I said to him, 'You're out of your mind, man. I know you're a great football player, but nobody's worth that kind of money.' And Joe put down his pool cue and looked at me with that sly smile of his and said, 'Gaylon, my attorneys tell me we're just getting started.'

"So every night when we'd go and play pool I'd ask, 'Okay, Joe, what's it up to today?' And then he'd tell me about those $20,000 and $30,000 jumps."

And that's pretty much what happened. At the very end the Cardinals actually offered Joe more money, but by then he and Sonny Werblin were the best of friends, and Werblin convinced

Joe he could make a lot more money from endorsements and other outside investments if he came to New York.

Even after Joe signed his contract, two obstacles had to be overcome before he could go to his first training camp as a member of the New York Jets—his bad right knee and the U.S. Army. Of the two, his injured knee was the easiest to surmount.

The operation was performed by Dr. James Nicholas, the team surgeon for the Jets, almost as soon as the Orange Bowl was over. No problem. Joe called right after the operation. Did it hurt much, I wanted to know?

"Heck no, Mom," he said. "I didn't feel a thing. But as soon as I woke up, Dr. Nicholas told me to start lifting my right leg. I thought he was kidding, but he said I had to start getting it back in shape right away. Now that did hurt."

The army trouble hurt even more.

Joe had been drafted, and like every good American boy he went down to the induction center, the one in New York, and took his physical. He didn't pass. He was rated 4-F because of his bad knee.

Well, I just couldn't believe the stink people raised. They couldn't understand how a big, tough football player like Joe could be unfit for military service. He got a lot of "fan" mail calling him a coward, a draft dodger, and even worse things than that. He wasn't the only professional athlete who was 4-F, not by a long shot, but people really jumped all over him. I didn't understand what all the fuss was about, but I guess it was that those same qualities Sonny Werblin said made him a star also polarized people's attitudes about him, right from the beginning of his professional career. People either loved him or hated him, even though most of his enemies had never even met him. I'm going to talk about this some more later on, because I think it's one of the most interesting aspects of Joe, but in 1965, with the army thing, Joe simply got a bad rap.

Joe was willing to go along with whatever the army decided. Because of all the publicity Joe's case received, the army made him take the physical three times, and all three times the results were the same. Joe could have tried to pull some strings, but he didn't, and finally the Surgeon General of the United States issued a special report that said exactly what three sets of army doctors had said: Joe's knees just weren't good enough for military service. The public outcry didn't die down for the and worse couldn't possibly have known that his sister, Rita, had served in the armed forces and that one of his brothers, Sonny, had made the army his life. Sonny, in fact, tried to enlist near the end of World War II, although he was much too young. He later served in Korea, and at the time Joe was having his problems, he was in Viet Nam. Bobby was also in the army, as was Sharon, Sonny's wife, and my brother Paul. Deep down, I know all my children love America. If Joe had passed his physical—any one of the three—he would have served his country gladly. He got a raw deal from the public, but it wouldn't be his last.

The first preseason training camp Joe attended was at the Peekskill Military Academy, not too far up the Hudson River from New York City. It was a hot time for him, to say the least. If it wasn't the July sun getting to him, it was the other players. Veteran players don't like rookies very much to begin with— those collegians are a real threat to their job security—and they like rich rookies even less. All of the veterans on the Jets knew about Joe's contract, of course, and a few of them were pretty resentful. I don't think their fight was with Joe personally, but here was a guy who'd never played a game of professional football in his life making more money for signing one contract than some of them would make in their entire careers.

I really wasn't too concerned over the fact that some of the players didn't like Joe. Those good ole boys at Alabama sure weren't in love with him at first either, but he sucked in his gut and stuck it out, and by the time he was a senior his teammates had voted him their offensive captain. Joe had shown he could handle himself, and I knew he would eventually be accepted by his new Jet teammates. It was just a matter of time.

But for a while, it was a very depressing time. Finally, just before the team broke camp, there was a special meeting just for the players. No coaches, no front office types, nobody except the players. Everybody was given a chance to air his gripes in an effort to clear the air. Joe later told me he was pretty choked up about the whole thing, but finally he stood up and, as he wrote in his own book, said to his teammates, "Some of you guys don't like me, but I don't care 'cause I don't like you. I mean, I don't know you very well, so I can't really like you or dislike you, but from the way you act, I don't like you.

72   All I'm asking is that you don't judge me for the money or the publicity, that you let me get out on the field and play football. If you dislike me for anything other than the money, tell me now. Let me know. If worse comes to worse, we'll do something about it—whatever way we have to."*

That was a pretty gutsy speech. Joe's a big guy and all, but if "worse came to worse" I don't honestly know how he would have made out against some of those huge linemen. It served its purpose, however. From that day on, whatever complaints Joe's teammates had about the money he was making were kept to themselves. Joe was allowed to become no more and no less than what he wanted to be—a part of his team.

Now the big question, of course, is whether Joe really was worth all that money. As his mother, my inclination was to say no, he wasn't.

He was worth more than he got, a lot more. And here's why.

Professional football is a sport, sure, but it's also a big-business entertainment, maybe the number one entertainment in the United States right now, and the people who get paid the most in the entertainment field are the ones who draw the crowds. Maybe you don't even have to be the best at what you do, but if you've got that charisma, or crowd appeal—what Sonny Werblin calls "star quality"—then people will fall all over themselves to come see you perform. To me, Joe is a mischievous, loving son and he always will be, but to a whole lot of football fans, he's somebody they love to hate and hate to love. Either way, they'll pay money for the privilege. As the person who keeps those turnstiles turning and cash registers jangling, Joe deserves a piece of the action. He does today and he certainly did in 1965. It was that simple.

How important was Joe's presence to the Jets' franchise and to the entire American Football League? It's hard to tell, but consider the fact that just a few years before Joe became a Jet, the team wasn't worth anything. Nothing at all. When the franchise was known as the New York Titans—they didn't become the Jets until 1960—the players didn't know from one week to the next whether they were going to get a paycheck.

---

*Joe Willie Namath with Dick Schaap, *I Can't Wait Until Tomorrow. . . 'Cause I Get Better—Looking Every Day* (New York: Random House, Inc., 1969) p. 163.

And when they did get one, they ran with it to the bank to see how high it would bounce. They didn't know whether their game uniforms would be cleaned, because nobody had the money to pay the laundry bills. They sometimes didn't even know if they would have footballs to practice with.

All of that changed long before Joe came to New York, of course, but in 1965 it was still touch and go whether the Jets and a whole lot of other teams would ever make it into the black. In the early 1960s, the old, established NFL was out to destroy the AFL, and because it had the prestige—and most of the television money—it might have succeeded if it hadn't been for the guts and brilliance of people like Lamar Hunt of the Kansas City Chiefs, Al Davis of the Oakland Raiders, and Sonny Werblin. In order for the league to survive, they all realized it had to put a good product on the field, one that people would want to come and see. And they all realized a good product costs a lot of money. In all honesty, I suppose if Joe Namath had never existed, the AFL still would have made it, but he just happened to be the right person in the right place at the right time—Joe's always been like that—and he took advantage of the opportunity.

At the same time, the Jets took advantage of Joe, in the nicest sense of that word. Just consider some of these figures: In 1964, the year before Joe came to New York, the Jets sold 22,000 season tickets and averaged 42,710 in paid attendance for each of their seven home games; in 1965, the respective figures were 39,000 and 54,877. At five dollars per average ticket per game, was Joe worth $427,000 for roughly three years' service? You figure it out. I did, and I calculated the Jets got their money back on Joe his very first season with the team.

Joe's entertainment value is just one point. What the AFL owners really wanted to do was force a merger with the NFL, both to ensure the stability of their own franchises and to get a slice of all that television money. When the NFL owners saw what the bidding war was doing to their pocketbooks—the fight for Joe Namath was the key in all of this—they decided enough was enough and, in 1966, agreed to merge, although the merger didn't fully take effect until the 1970 season. What did that do to the value of the Jets' franchise? Well, in 1963, Sonny Werblin and his group bought the Jets for $1 million. In 1969, when they were champions of the world, the Jets were worth over $16 million. Now you couldn't buy the Jets for anything less than maybe $22 million, if that. Was Joe worth his $427,000? You figure it out some more. Sonny Werblin's a fine gentleman, but I think he got himself a bargain.

From the players' point of view, there is also another point to be made. When all those angry veterans learned what Joe was making even before he'd played his first pro game, they went right back to the owners and started renegotiating their own contracts. Remember when Larry Bruno, Joe's high school coach, was offered that bonus contract of $125 by the Pittsburgh Steelers in 1946? Well, that was a long time ago, practically in the dark ages of pro football. But in 1964 the average salary of a professional player was just over $20,000; today it's up to almost $50,000, and the Player's Association is currently asking for a *minimum* salary of $20,000 for rookies and $25,000 for veterans. There are a whole lot of stars in the National Football League making more money than Joe did even in 1974. Joe's teammates may have resented him when he first joined the Jets, but the publicity his contract generated eventually made all of them a whole lot richer, too.

Yet another consideration is that no professional athlete has a very long career, but the length of a professional football player's career is especially short. Oh, there are always some players around who seem to go on forever, like that fellow George Blanda over at Oakland. He'll probably still be playing when Joe's a grandfather. Or Fran Tarkenton, who's played for fourteen years now and hasn't even broken a fingernail. But those are the exceptions that prove the rule. The average career of an NFL player lasts only around five years. Why? The competition from the rookies gets tougher every year. I don't know what they feed them in college these days, but each season the players seem to be bigger, stronger, and faster, and if you make it past your second year, you're either very, very good—or very, very lucky, because a pro football player's career can end at any time. Joe is fortunate to have played for ten years. His career would be over tomorrow if he stepped off the sidewalk wrong and his knees just fell apart forever. Football is a rough game and every player knows the first contract he signs may be his last, no matter how good he is. For every George Blanda around, there are always five or six Gayle Sayer's—fine, fine ballplayers cut down by injuries even before they reached their prime. Even Tucker Frederickson had only one or two good years before injuries started to wreck his career—and his earning power.

Sometimes players never get a chance in the pros. For example, quarterback Jimmy Sidle, a high school all-American with Joe and a teammate of Frederickson's at Auburn in 1963, was a college all-American whose future looked every bit as bright as Joe's. But in the first game of his senior year he injured his shoulder and never did get a chance at the big money. I firmly believe every professional athlete, especially a football player, deserves all the money he can get just as fast as he can get it.

And finally, Joe turned out to be a pretty fair country quarterback, although you never would have known it for a while. The Jets had four quarterbacks in camp that first year, Jim Turner, Mike Taliaferro, John Huarte, and Joe. Maybe Sonny Werblin thought Joe was a star, but Weeb Ewbank, the head coach, had a team to worry about and he knew that rookies just don't come into the pros and set the world on fire. At least not right away. When the exhibition season began, Taliaferro was the number one quarterback, and Joe was the number two quarterback. Joe's first start was against Buffalo, a team that would win the AFL championship that year, and I thought he was marvelous. He completed nineteen of forty passes for 282 yards and two touchdowns. But Buffalo won, and all Joe said afterward was, "I'm disgusted. I learned to win in high school and college, and that's what I want to do in the pros."

When the regular season began, Joe and Taliaferro sort of alternated as the number one quarterback. Joe was erratic. He'd come in and throw a touchdown pass, then he'd throw an interception. Never before in their history had the Jets been more than barely respectable, and with the 1965 season well under way, their record was a miserable 0–4–1. But on October 24, in the sixth game of the year, against a powerful San Diego team, suddenly it all seemed to fall in place for Joe: what a pro quarterback was expected to do and how he should go about doing it. With the Jets trailing badly and with just five minutes left to go, Joe was sent in. Although nothing miraculous happened and the Jets lost again, Joe said later those five minutes were the turning point of his rookie year. In his own mind he had established himself as a professional quarter-back—and hardly anybody noticed.

Two weeks later, however, against Kansas City, everybody noticed. Taliaferro again started, but near the end of the first half both Joe and Coach Ewbank spotted a weakness in the Kansas City secondary that just begged for exploitation with a series of short little passes. Ewbank told Taliaferro to throw short, but Mike continued to heave long bombs that got the Jets nowhere. In the second half Ewbank sent Joe in, and Joe immediately began picking the Chiefs apart with . . . short little passes. The result was a 13–10 upset for the Chiefs, and from that day on Joe was the Jets' starting quarterback.

Two weeks later, Joe had his best day ever as a quarter-back—in high school, college, or the pros—when he completed seventeen of twenty-six passes for four touchdowns as the Jets amassed 522 yards in total offense enroute to a 41–14 win over Houston. Joe had arrived.

The win over the Oilers was the Jets' fourth straight, and with a season-closing upset of Buffalo, they ended the 1965 season with a 5–8–1 record. At the end of the year, Joe ranked third among the AFL quarterbacks with 164 completions in 340 attempts for 2,220 yards. He threw eighteen touchdown passes that year and—I hate to even mention this—fifteen intercep-tions. He surprised all of his critics by being named the AFL's Rookie of the Year in a landslide, getting eighteen of the twenty-four first-place votes that were cast.

In the AFL all-star game, Joe had another good day, and afterward Sid Gillman, coach of the league-champion Buffalo Bills, said, "In three or four years Joe Namath is going to be one of the greatest quarterbacks in pro football history."

Coach Gillman was a smart cookie, because that's exactly what happened. Joe continued his education as a pro quarter-back over the next two seasons. There were good days and bad days—more good than bad—and through it all the Jets were putting together one fine football team. Joe brought me to several games and I could tell by just talking to the players they were really a close bunch of guys. They stuck up for each other, they were happy, and more important, they were improving every week. They were getting closer to the top, but just how close I had no idea. In 1966 their record was 6–6–2 and in 1967 it was 8–5–1, but for me it was fun enough just to sit back on those Sunday afternoons with my family and friends and watch the Jets play, knowing the fellow wearing that green and white jersey with No. 12 on it was my son Joe.

If I had had a crystal ball before the 1968 season began, maybe I could have seen the signs. After the accident against North Carolina State, Joe never again failed to tape his shoes for support. They became sort of his trademark, but the Jets' front office did Joe one better: they bought him a special pair of white kangaroo-hide shoes for his very own. It was a small thing, but it indicated to me how much they really thought of him.

Then, just before the regular season was to begin, one of the assistant coaches came to Joe with a big grin on his face and said, "Joe, you've just been elected the offensive captain of the New York Jets."

That was probably the happiest moment in Joe's life. It meant that he had finally been accepted as a member of the Jets. He had come a long way—or maybe the Jets had—since that day in his first training camp when he felt he had to ask his teammates to accept him for what he was and not just as another rich rookie. Now he was a part of them, no questions asked, and the Jets were ready to take off.

I really felt that 1968 was going to be the Jets' best year ever. But since I didn't have that crystal ball, I couldn't possibly have known just how good. It turned out that a lot of other people didn't have a very good crystal ball, either.

I should have known, though. Just before the first game of the regular season, Joe told me with a wink, "You can expect big things from us this year, Mom," and Joe never lies.

SIX

Although the Jets had been getting better and better during Joe's three years with the team—and in 1967 had finished just one game behind Houston in the Eastern Division of the AFL—nobody picked them to win anything in 1968. I guess there were a lot of good reasons, at least on paper. Several of the Jets had been injured in 1967, including those bruising running backs Matt Snell and Emerson Boozer, and nobody could say how well they would play in 1968 or for how long. And by now, both of Joe's knees were giving him trouble. Since the very afternoon he hurt his right knee in college, he had tended to depend more on the left, so much so that in 1966 it began to go as well. That kind of thing happens a lot, I understand, but for a while his left knee was so painful he had a hard time just walking down a flight of stairs. It killed me to see him in constant pain. The doctors told him he should be sure and wrap his left knee even before he played a round of golf, let alone a football game. And there had been two more operations—a second one on his right knee in late 1966 and one on his left knee in early 1968.

So in the Eastern Division the favorite was Houston. That didn't make much difference, though, because all the experts decided beforehand that whoever won in the East would surely lose to the Western Division champions, either Kansas City or Oakland, in the playoffs. And even *that* didn't make any difference, because, of course, the AFL champions would just get clobbered by the NFL champions—the experts picked the Baltimore Colts and it's nice to report they were right about something—in the Super Bowl. After all, hadn't the Green Bay Packers of the NFL easily won the first two Super Bowls over Kansas City and Oakland? Surely the 1968 season would be more of the same.

But in the very first game of the year, Joe showed that maybe those so-called experts were in for a long year. Against the powerful Kansas City Chiefs, Joe had a brilliant first half that put the Jets into a commanding 17–3 lead, and late in the fourth quarter Jim Turner kicked a field goal to provide the margin of victory in a 20–19 win.

In their second game the Jets went wild and gleefully overwhelmed Boston, 47–31, and I didn't need a crystal ball to see the Jets were already something special.

The very next week, however, I began to wonder. Against Buffalo, as Joe later told a writer, "I completed twenty-four passes—nineteen to the Jets and five to the Bills," and Buffalo came away with a 37–35 victory. After another win, poor Joe had a second miserable afternoon, this time against the then lowly Denver Broncos. Another five interceptions helped the Broncs to an upset win, and after five games the Jets' record was a so-so three wins, two losses. Maybe the prognosticators were right after all.

Four games later, though, the Jets stood at 7–2, just like that, and with Houston, the team the experts said would win the Eastern Division, stumbling along at 4–6, it looked like the Jets were a shoo-in to win the first divisional title in their history.

Joe was having a great year, but certainly a strange one. In six straight games, Joe had failed to throw a touchdown pass and I was getting a little worried. I'm no expert, just a mother, but I did know enough to realize that quarterbacks, especially quarterbacks with big salaries, are supposed to throw touchdowns. And here my Joey had gone almost half a season without throwing one.

But the person that counted, Joe, wasn't worried at all. He said all those armchair experts just didn't know what pro football was all about.

"We're winning, Mom, and that's what counts," he said. "I don't care if I never throw a touchdown pass as long as my team's ahead when the final gun goes off."

Now I knew for sure the Jets were something special. And so was Joe. He didn't care about himself at all, only his team. Just the way it should be.

Well, like the man says, nothing is ever sure in this life except death and taxes, and in the tenth game of the year the Jets and the Oakland Raiders hooked up in just about the craziest football game ever played. My girlfriends and I went over to watch the game at Aunt Anna's house—she's the widow of my late brother, Joe Juhasz—while we played a couple of games of 500 gin rummy. The football game went back and forth and back and forth with both Joe and Daryle Lamonica, the Oakland quarterback, just having a field day throwing that football around. It was a fun afternoon. We were rooting and cheering between deals, and when Jim Turner kicked a thirty-two-yard field goal to put the Jets ahead, 32–29, with only sixty-eight seconds left, all of us were beside ourselves with glee.

Then the television set went blank, and out of nowhere this little girl by the name of Heidi started skipping across the Swiss countryside. Promptly at 7 p.m. somebody at NBC had pulled the plug on the most exciting football game of the year to show a children's program, and there we were along with the rest of America wondering what on earth was going on. But, we thought, there's only a minute to go. What can possibly happen? We all got comfortable and dealt out another hand.

But after a few minutes I said, "Wait a minute. I know the Jets had to win, but I'm going to call up the radio station just to make sure of the final score."

All the other women watched as I dialed the number. Then the man at the station said, "Rose, you'll never believe what happened. The Jets lost by eleven points."

Lost? By *eleven points*? It was impossible. I hung up the phone and just started hollering, "They lost. They lost. I can't believe it." If there had been a big hole handy, I would have jumped right in. It was a catastrophe.

In those last sixty-eight seconds, Oakland had scored a quick touchdown on its own, then scored another touchdown when a Jet back fumbled the kickoff in the end zone and a Raider fell on it. Joe had completed nineteen of thirty-seven passes for 381 yards, but that didn't make any difference at all. The Jets had lost the *Heidi* Bowl, 43–32, and still hadn't clinched the divisional title. I didn't feel much like playing cards any more.

But two weeks later on December 1—just about the time the switchboard at NBC finally quieted down—the Jets beat Miami, 35–17, with two games remaining in the regular season, and finally nailed down their Eastern championship.

Two other little things happened that month of December. That was the year Joe first grew his Fu Manchu mustache. I thought it was pretty cute, but the people who ran the AFL decided long hair and mustaches presented a bad image of the professional football player—as though you could tell a person's character by the length of his hair—and told everybody in the league to take it off, take it all off. Especially Joe.

Joe and his teammates refused until they clinched the championship. Then a nice company that makes razor blades offered Joe $10,000 if he would take it off with one of their razor blades on national television. Joe did, in what must have been the most expensive mustache trim in the history of the world.

Then, just before the Jets' final game of the year, also against Miami, Joe received a great honor from his teammates. He was elected their most valuable player for the first time. Miami didn't have a chance. Joe played only the first half as the Jets won easily, 31–7, and prepared to face Oakland for the championship of the AFL.

Here we go with the experts again. Mainly because they had won so stunningly in the *Heidi* Bowl, the Raiders were made a slight favorite. By now the New York-Oakland rivalry was one of the most intense in the young history of the newer league. There had always been bad blood between those two teams. In a game the previous year, Oakland's huge defensive end, Ben Davidson, had come crashing through Joe's usually reliable blockers and put an elbow up inside Joe's face mask with such force it dislodged Joe's helmet and almost knocked him out. Joe stayed in the game—in fact, he threw two more touchdown passes—and didn't learn until afterwards that Davidson had broken his cheekbone. The broken cheekbone was just one of those things that happen every now and again. However, the incident only served to make a bitter rivalry even more bitter, and now, more than a year later, the two clubs were going to play one game that might mean as much as $25,000 per player plus the prestige of an appearance in the Super Bowl.

This time the game was played in New York at Shea Stadium on a miserable, cold, and windy afternoon before more than 62,000 miserable, cold people. Just like the *Heidi* game, this one turned into a real donnybrook, too.

Right away New York got off to a great start. The first time the Jets got the ball, Joe took them by bits and pieces down inside the Oakland twenty-yard line and from there threw a little fourteen-yard pass to Don Maynard. When Jim Turner kicked a thirty-three-yard field goal a few minutes later, the New York lead was up to 10–0.

But Daryle Lamonica was having some fun, too. He led Oakland to one touchdown, and after an exchange of field goals the New York lead at half time was just three points, 13–10.

In the third period the old man, George Blanda, kicked a second field goal to tie the game at 13–13, and it was obviously time for Joe to go to work again. He let Matt Snell and Emerson Boozer carry the ball most of the way to the Oakland twenty, then threw a beautiful clothesline pass between two Raider defensive backs. Pete Lammons caught it for another touchdown. The score: New York 20, Oakland 13.

George Blanda got his old leg working again, however, to reduce the Jets' lead to four points, 20–16, and early in the fourth quarter the Raiders scored a touchdown to go ahead for the first time, 23–20.

Watching the game on television, I was beside myself. I hoped for two things: for NBC not to cut off the end of the game and for Joe to get another touchdown. NBC cooperated and so did Joe. He threw a long pass to Don Maynard, who played the entire game with an injured leg, that moved the ball from the New York forty-two all the way down to the Oakland six. On the next play Joe found himself boxed in and for a few terrifying seconds it looked as though he'd have to eat the football, as they say. But out of the corner of his eye he saw that marvelous Don Maynard slip loose in the end zone. Joe threw the ball and Don caught it skidding on his knees. A few minutes later when the Jets recovered a loose Oakland lateral deep in their territory, they had the championship, 27–23, and Joe, who had said just over three years earlier that he'd been a winner in high school and college and expected to be one in the pros, too, was just that.

Now it was time for the Super Bowl and to see whether Joe could confound those so-called experts again.

The Super Bowl was going to be played in Miami, and I was dying to go. I'd had a ball four years earlier when Alabama and Texas played that great Orange Bowl game, and Joe signed that great contract. But when it came time to make plans for the trip south, Joe's brothers found a million reasons for me to stay home. They pointed out that I was nervous about flying. They said I could get hijacked to Cuba. They said it might rain. All sorts of excuses. But I think the real reason was that they didn't want me running around Miami shooting off my mouth in defense of Joe.

From what the newspapers said, it sounded as though Joe could have used a couple of good lawyers down there. In the two weeks before the game, it seemed like every time he opened his mouth he said something designed to get those Baltimore Colts, the NFL champions, all riled up to the point they couldn't even see straight.

It all began when those so-called experts came out and picked Baltimore to win the Super Bowl by seventeen points. I must admit, being slightly prejudiced, that when I first heard the point spread, I thought New York was favored. Then Franklin explained that no, the Colts were. Right then and there I knew those experts didn't know a thing about football. Baltimore had a good team, but there was no way it could beat New York, and certainly not by seventeen points.

Right away I made a few wagers—friendly wagers, you understand—with people right here in Beaver Falls. Now, most of the people in town were Jets' fans, of course, but just like the rest of the country, they were conned by the myth of National Football League superiority. Hadn't the NFL won the first two Super Bowls? Hadn't the NFL been around for more than forty years? Isn't old wine always better than new? I really jumped on those seventeen points, and it wasn't the first time I had placed a bet either. Back in the old days I would sometimes write down three numbers on a piece of paper and give them to Joey, along with a nickel, to take down to the nice man at the corner drugstore. It was a nice, friendly wager, playing the numbers, and sometimes I'd even win. And now, years later, I realize I may not have known a lot about football, but I sure knew a good bet when I saw one.

So maybe it was the ridiculous point spread that was causing Joe to do all his talking down in Miami—that and the fact Joe cannot tell a lie. Whenever the press people—and a lot of other people, too, as it turned out—asked Joe a question, he told them the truth. None of this, "Any team can win on any Sunday," or, "The Colts are sure gonna be tough," or, "We'll just have to see what happens," or, "It should be a good game." Joe is really a very modest fellow, but he's also very honest. Sometimes people get the two confused. Lou Michaels sure did.

Joe's little confrontation with Michaels was one of the three really controversial things he got mixed up with before the Super Bowl. As usual, the press got it all wrong. Joe told me later exactly what happened.

Both the Jets and the Colts practiced in Fort Lauderdale. The Jets, in fact, stayed at a hotel called the Galt Ocean Mile, the same one the Green Bay Packers had stayed in the year before, and Joe and his roommate, Jim Hudson, had the Governor's Suite, the same room Vince Lombardi had occupied. At any rate, it seems that one night Joe and Jim were recovering from practice at Jimmy Fazio's, a Fort Lauderdale watering hole, when Lou Michaels and Dan Sullivan, another Colt, walked in. Pretty soon Lou and Joe got to talking. Since Lou Michaels was the placekicker for the Colts, naturally, the subject of their conversation got around to the Super Bowl. It was a nice, friendly talk. Lou explained how the Colts were going to beat the Jets by thirty points or so, and Joe countered with the notion that Lou might possibly be in error and further suggested that he was full of beans. Or something.

Then the conversation got more personal. After a few more drinks, I think Joe said there might even have been some name-calling. And I do recall Joe mentioning that at one point he and Lou Michaels stood up across the table from each other before some friends stepped in and suggested they talk about the weather. And that's as far as it got. I found out later Joe even picked up the tab, and that the two men parted the best of friends.

That's all there was to it, but to read the papers the next day you'd have thought there had been a drunken brawl. That just wasn't true. First of all, Joe isn't so dumb that he'd go around picking fights with a 250-pound lineman. He calls every guard and tackle he meets, "Sir," whether they're friend or foe. And none of the stories, of course, mentioned that Lou Michaels was a friend of the family, that he and Joe's brother Franklin were roommates at the University of Kentucky, and that he had even visited Franklin a couple of times in Beaver Falls.

I think what happened is that the press didn't have enough to write about down there and were trying to generate some excitement by building up the game into some kind of Hate Bowl. They sure succeeded.

Then there was the day some newspaper people asked Joe what he thought about Earl Morrall, the Baltimore quarterback who had stepped in to replace Johnny Unitas early in the season and had been named the NFL's Most Valuable Player. Well, Joe's honesty got the best of him again. He told those writers there were at least four quarterbacks in the AFL better than Morrall.

"Who?" they asked.

"There's John Hadl of San Diego, Bob Griese of Miami, Daryle Lamonica of Oakland, and . . . me," he answered.

Well goodness gracious. That's something you just don't say about another team's quarterback before a big game. It's the kind of quote opposing coaches love to hang on the locker room wall to get their own players psyched up. Pro football is a game of skill and intelligence, but there's a lot of raw emotion involved, too. Weeb Ewbank, the Jets' coach, like to have died when he read what Joe had said. He tried to play it down, but as usual, Joe's frankness carried the day.

For sure, Joe kept Miami hopping those two weeks before the Super Bowl. But as the day of the game drew near, a semblance of normality was beginning to return around town—until the Thursday before the big day when Joe attended a banquet given by the Miami Touchdown Club honoring him as pro football's Player of the Year. And right there before God, Earl Morrall, and everybody, he made his famous pronouncement: "We're going to win the Super Bowl. I *guarantee* it." I could just see poor Weeb Ewbank sliding under the table as the press clippings in the Baltimore dressing room got fatter and fatter.

Joe knew what he was talking about. Baltimore had a 14–1 record going into the Super Bowl, and it was a team to be respected. In fact, before the Jets went to Miami, Joe wasn't sure himself the Jets could win. But "the one-eyed monster" told him they could.

In high school, Joe had taken a course to learn how to run a movie projector, and he didn't do it just to pick up a few easy credits. He knew that a quarterback, more than any other player on the team, always had to study the opposition. Before every Jet game he would spend long evenings in his own apartment running films of the upcoming Sunday's opponent, searching for one tiny flaw he might be able to exploit on the field when the time came.

He did the same thing with the Baltimore Colts. "I go with what the one-eyed monster shows me," he always liked to say. "The one-eyed monster doesn't lie. It tells it like it is." And it wasn't until he wore out those films of the Colts that he was ready to guarantee a Jets' victory.

And when he did, I knew the Jets were home free. Joe doesn't lie.

Still, I was worried. After all, Joe was my son, and I sure didn't want him getting all those big Baltimore linemen mad at him. But when I told him on the telephone to be a little more tactful, all he said was, "If the Colts need to use newspaper clippings to get fired up for a game, they're in trouble. Don't worry, Mom. Everything'll be all right." And then he winked again, right over the telephone.

Far away in Fort Knox, Kentucky, Sonny Namath, Joe's oldest brother, was also upholding the honor of the Jets. He was stationed there along with another soldier named Bruce Matte, the younger brother of the Baltimore running back, Tom Matte, and I understand they got into a few discussions about the Super Bowl just like Joe and Lou Michaels had done down in Miami. Sonny was just as confident as Joe, but in a more reasoned way. He kept telling Bruce, "Sure the Jets were lucky to beat Kansas City early in the season, and they were lucky to beat Oakland in the play-offs. But in the Super Bowl there won't be any luck involved, because the Jets play in a better league."

I was full of confidence, too, of course, but the day before the game I was a bundle of nerves. I did my grocery shopping for the weekend just like all of us good housewives, and then I spent the evening before the game watching television. But even after my husband Steve and I had gone to bed, I was so restless I couldn't sleep. I finally had to take a nerve pill and a couple of sleeping tablets—and before I knew it, it was morning: January 12, 1969.

I was working at Lane's Drugstore at the time, and Super Bowl Sunday was just like every other Sunday. I had to open the store at nine o'clock in the morning because we sold a lot of newspapers. I worked straight through lunch so Mr. Lane, the owner, could let me go home at two o'clock, an hour before the kickoff. Everybody who came into the store had something to say because they knew I was Joe Namath's mother, but I was surprised at the number of people who thought the Jets would lose. I guess people had their favorites, just like for every other big game, but I think some of those who told me they were Baltimore fans were just trying to pull my chain. That was okay, though; I gave it right back to them.

Instead of coming straight home, I walked over to St. Mary's Church. And you know? It was so funny. There wasn't a living soul on that street. It seemed like everybody was home just waiting for something to happen. I lit a candle and prayed to Saint Mary and to Saint Jude. Although the Blessed Mother is my favorite, I seem to have more luck with Saint Mary. She listens to me more.

When I got home there was just Steve and me and Joe's dog Sammy. We didn't eat, we didn't drink, we didn't do anything except walk up and down the living room, the dining room, and the kitchen waiting for that game to start. Steve was worse than I was. He just kept pacing and pacing until finally I yelled at him, "For God's sake, sit down. You're making *me* nervous." Only Sammy, the dog, was calm. He couldn't understand what all the excitement was about. He kept looking at me like he was thinking, "What's the matter with you? Don't you have any trust in your own son? Well, I do. And I'm going to sleep."

And that's exactly what happened. Joe's dog curled up behind the couch and slept through the entire Super Bowl.

Actually, I did feel pretty confident—nervous but confident. I'm not one to believe in numbers or magic, but the game was being played on the twelfth and Joe wore No. 12. That had to be a good sign, didn't it? An even better sign was that the Jets were wearing white. The fellows in white were always the good guys, weren't they? Finally, when Joe and Johnny Sample, the

Jets' captains, walked out on the field and won the toss of the coin, I knew everything would be okay.

The game didn't start out okay, though. The Colts dominated the game all through the first quarter and right into the second, just like the experts said they would. The Jets took the opening kickoff and picked up one first down. Then they punted, and right away the Colts looked like they were going to put some points on the scoreboard. In only five plays Baltimore moved to the New York nineteen-yard line, first and ten.

Earl Morrall, however, came through brilliantly for the Jets. He missed two passes in a row and then got thrown for a loss. Maybe Joe was right after all. Maybe Earl Morrall wasn't the best quarterback around.

Then Lou Michaels came on to try a field goal from the twenty-seven, a pretty short distance when you've been kicking the ball around as long as Lou has. But he missed. Maybe it was the pressure of all those 73,000 fans in the Orange Bowl yelling and screaming, or maybe Saint Mary had listened to me, but Lou Michaels missed, and it was the last time he showed up on the field until it didn't matter anymore.

The rest of the first quarter both teams played pretty conservative football, but back in Beaver Falls I was going crazy. Every time there was a time out I went into the kitchen and beat on the walls, just praying for the Jets to get something going, but it never happened. Just the opposite, in fact. Near the end of the first quarter Joe completed a pass from deep in his own territory to George Sauer, who fumbled the ball after being hit hard by Baltimore's Lenny Lyles. The Colts recovered on the New York twelve-yard line.

Then a couple of plays later that nice Earl Morrall came through again. Morrall saw his tight end Tom Mitchell wide open in the end zone. He threw the ball, but Jets' middle linebacker Al Atkinson made a great play and deflected the pass into the arms of Jets' cornerback Randy Beverly.

My son had been given a second reprieve and at last he was ready to take advantage of it—with the help of that "one-eyed monster." There were two technical reasons why Joe knew the Jets would beat the Colts. First, the left offensive tackle for the Jets, Winston Hill, often would be matched up against Ordell Braase, the left defensive end of the Colts, and Joe knew the younger and quicker Hill could beat his older and slower rival.

Second, the key to the Baltimore defense was its ability to blitz opposing quarterbacks. It had worked well in the NFL, but Joe knew that with his quick release he could dump passes into the area vacated by the blitz almost at will.

With those two considerations in mind, Joe went to work. Matt Snell slammed into the line behind Winston Hill for short but consistent yardage, and Joe threw those quickie passes; after a while New York was on the Baltimore four. In the huddle Joe called a "19-straight," which was Snell's number. The hole that was supposed to be open for Matt was there and he stormed into the end zone. At last! The extra point made the score New York 7, Baltimore 0, and for the first time in three Super Bowls the AFL team led the NFL representative.

Right near the end of the second period Earl Morrall came through a third time for the Jets. He threw the bomb, but instead of aiming at Jimmy Orr, who was wide open and signaling frantically, he tossed it to John Mackey, who was covered, and the pass was intercepted by Joe's roomie, Jim Hudson.

In the third quarter the Jets got their first real break of the game when Tom Matte fumbled in Baltimore territory. A few minutes later Jim Turner kicked a field goal. Now the score was New York 10, Baltimore 0.

Later in the same period, with the Jets on the march again, Joe dropped back and threw a hard pass to Don Maynard in the end zone. Don caught it, but the referees said he was out of the end zone. I hardly noticed. Upfield, my son Joe was grimacing with pain. As he released the ball he had slammed his hand against the shoulder pads of Baltimore tackle Fred Miller, and it was obvious his hand was hurt. Joe ran to the sidelines and Babe Parelli, New York's backup quarterback, came in for two plays. Then a big sigh of relief went up in the Orange Bowl—and in my living room as well—as Joe trotted back out on the field just in time for Jim Turner to kick another field goal that lengthened the Jets lead to 13–0.

At the start of the final fifteen minutes, Turner again did his thing. Now the score was 16–0 and Baltimore needed a miracle. I knew for sure all my bets were safe, and I knew for sure the Jets had the game won—and oh my, what a great big sigh of relief I let out. I wasn't even worried when Johnny Unitas replaced Earl Morrall. He's a great guy and a marvelous quarterback, but all's fair in a Super Bowl. I didn't think Johnny Unitas could do any more than my Joe. I wasn't afraid of the name.

Unitas did get Baltimore one touchdown, but midway through that last quarter the Jets intercepted him. Joe coolly didn't try to score any more points but just used up the clock. He stayed on the ground for eight straight plays, and the Jets retained possession for nearly five crucial minutes.

And then the New York Jets were the football champions of the world.

Joe called me after the game as soon as he could. I think he was still in the dressing room. He didn't have much to say, because Joe never was one to brag about winning a football game, even the Super Bowl.

"Hiya, Mom," he said. "Did you like the game?"

"I sure did, honey," I said. "It was wonderful. It was just a beautiful game."

I could tell he was proud and happy, for himself and for his teammates.

The celebration in Beaver Falls went on most of the night, but all Steve and I did was sit down and eat our chicken dinner, although with the phone ringing so much I'm surprised I didn't burn that bird right up.

Did the phone ring a lot after the game? Why, it rang so much for one whole week I didn't have time to do the dishes. Everybody in Beaver Falls either called or stopped by to give Joe and me their best, and I must have received three cartons of mail at the house in Joe's name.

Despite all the nervousness of watching that game, I really did know from the start the Jets were going to win. Not just because my son was their quarterback, but because Joe told me they were going to win—and Joe never lies.

SEVEN

At the age of twenty-five, Joe had the whole world in the palm of his hand. He had overcome a childhood somewhat less than overflowing with opportunity, a series of injuries and other hard knocks that might have discouraged a lesser man, the resentment of teammates both at the University of Alabama and on the New York Jets, and a number of bad raps in the press. Now he stood at the pinnacle of his career as the quarterback of the best team in professional football. It seemed only natural that he should be honored by the folks in the city where it all began.

And so on May 24, 1969, exactly one week before Joe's twenty-sixth birthday, the first, and maybe the last, "Joe Namath Day" was celebrated by the good burghers of Beaver Falls, Pennsylvania. Since that sad, frantic day nearly eight years earlier when Joe had left for Tuscaloosa, he had returned home many times, of course. But mainly these were quiet visits, an opportunity for Joe to see his family and catch up on the local news. This time, however, he was arriving as the conquering hero, the local boy who makes good, and neither I nor anybody else in Beaver Falls really had any idea of what to expect. Which was probably a good thing.

Joe flew into the Pittsburgh airport. When he got off the plane, it looked as though the celebration had already started. There was Joe, of course, dressed immaculately in a soft green suit that just matched his sleepy, green eyes. Then the rest of his entourage disembarked and they just kept coming: his lawyers Jimmy Walsh and Mike Bite, various teammates from both the University of Alabama and the New York Jets, Coach Bear Bryant of Alabama and Coach Weeb Ewbank of the Jets (there was a study in contrast—the big, tall Bear next to the short, rotund Weeb), some public relations men, several photographers and writers, and finally, two young ladies. A short one and a tall one. The tall one was gorgeous—I can't think of any other word to adequately describe her—and the short one was, well, stunning. She was wearing one of those blouses you can see right through, and believe me, there was plenty to see right through at. Right away I began to feel nervous; not exactly because of her, but because of what the folks in Beaver Falls would think. They had already heard plenty of crazy stories about Joe, and I could just imagine the new gossip when she showed up on Joe's arm.

There was an unofficial reception committee in Pittsburgh waiting for Joe—about a hundred teen-age girls who somehow had found out when his plane was arriving. They all stood off to one side tittering and jumping up and down, until one of them made a mad dash for Joe that set off a miniature mob scene, and made me wonder whether the first "Joe Namath Day" would ever make it past the airport.

Finally, though, the entourage got under way. Joe rode in the first limousine to Beaver Falls with his father, John, and Larry Bruno, his high school coach, who was the chairman of the "Joe Namath Day" festivities. I would like to interject something right here about both men. Although Joe's father and I were separated many years ago and have both since remarried, Joe remains very close to both of us. John was at the Super Bowl, and one of the great pictures to come out of that wonderful afternoon was one showing the two of them hugging each other in the locker room after the game. I am very glad and thankful for their continued relationship. It has been good for both of them. As for Larry Bruno, what can I say? Joe was obviously the most prominent athlete Larry ever coached, and as Joe got more famous, more controversial, and more successful, it would have been understandable if he had taken advantage of their association. He never did. In fact, even today the only memento of Joe in Coach Bruno's office is a small, eight-by-ten black and white picture of Joe—with Bear Bryant. That's it. Coach Bruno is just as self-effacing now as he was when Joe was his quarterback, and I think he deserves a lot of credit for staying that way. A lot of men wouldn't have.

At any rate, the caravan of four cars—Beaver Falls isn't a rich town and finding even a single limousine was difficult until one of the town's funeral parlors came through—drove northwest from the airport up through the Beaver Valley. It passed through Ambridge, Aliquippa, Freedom, and Monaca, and just before it got to Beaver Falls, it passed through Rochester. Already the memories and the ironies were starting to flood in, just as they would for the rest of the day. Rochester, remember, was the hometown of Babe Parelli. When Joey was only ten years old, Parelli was already playing professional football, after an illustrious college career at Kentucky under Bear Bryant. Several years later when Joe wound up playing for Coach Bryant at Alabama, the Bear shocked quite a few people down south by saying, "Joe is the best quarterback I've ever coached, and that includes Babe Parelli." Then, of course, Parelli finished out his career with the Jets, where he was Joe's backup during the year of the Super Bowl triumph. It's sometimes not a very big world after all.

When the caravan reached Beaver Falls, it stopped at Sahli Chevrolet and everybody transferred to convertibles for the police-escorted parade through town. I couldn't help but chuckle at that, too, because the last time Joe left Sahli Chevrolet it had also been with the encouragement of the police—the night he and some high school football teammates had tried to capture that helium-filled advertising balloon and decorate it with the Beaver Falls High School colors.

Then the parade drove around the block and passed the house on Sixth Street where Joe had spent his early childhood. It wasn't hard at all for me to recall how Joe had formed his first friendships from among the black kids in the neighborhood, or to remember the rock fights, pickup football games, and all his other mischievous adventures of those years. It seemed like only yesterday when he and his brothers and sister were terrorizing the whole block—and each other—with the exuberance of their youth. The Broadway Joe of 1969 lived in a whole different world from the one he grew up in, and I wondered then how he remembered his early years.

We passed by the various places where the partners in Namath & Alford Enterprises had gotten their introduction to the world of business. And Lord, we even passed by the trestle where Joey and Linny had scared the daylights out of Mrs. Alford and me that summer day so many years ago. I wished fervently that Linny could have been there, but he was serving his country in Viet Nam. (Linny told me much later he had listened to the Super Bowl in Saigon on the Armed Services Radio Network. He predicted the Jets would win, but before the game none of his buddies believed him; after the game none of his buddies believed he knew Joe Namath.)

When the parade turned up Seventh Avenue, the main street of Beaver Falls, I was stunned. We had expected maybe 2,000 or 3,000 people at the most—after all, the city only has a population of 14,500—but I was told there were over 25,000 people lining the sidewalks, just to see Joe. Kids from all over the place dashed up to besiege Joe and the others for autographs on baseball gloves, footballs, tiny scraps of paper, and just about anything else they could get their hands on. Joe accommodated them all, as he usually does, but I think he must have had writer's cramp long before the parade ended.

After the parade Joe and his friends went out to the Holiday Inn to freshen up, and I was given a ride back down Seventh Avenue to my home in Patterson Heights. As I've said, that's one of the nicer sections of the Beaver Falls area, and I never dreamed I'd ever be living there—especially when I was working as a maid for that nice doctor at a dollar a day—but the year before, Joe had bought a modest, comfortable house for me on Ross Hill Road, and I wanted to make sure everything was ready for his real homecoming.

I had spent several days making a beautiful sign to put up across the front porch railing, and as I walked into the front yard I couldn't help but admire my handiwork. In New York Jets' green I had painted a literary masterpiece: "Welcome Home Mommie's Hero!"

Well, my goodness, you should have heard the uproar about an hour later when Joe arrived with some of his Jets teammates. Even before they walked through the door I heard somebody mimic, *"Welcome home, Mommie's hero."*

I looked outside and saw Joe taking down my sign. "Gee, Mom," he said. "I was kind of thinking that maybe we shouldn't advertise this hero business so much."

I was undaunted. After Joe and the others had sat down to a light snack I'd prepared, I put the sign back up.

Joe was undaunted, too. He took the sign down a second time—and hid it in the garage. I let the matter ride until Joe left town. Then I put it back up and this time it stayed up until the weather took it down. I was proud of my work and I still am.

That night there was a banquet for Joe at the Geneva College field house. More than a thousand people turned out to honor Joe. The decorations were out of this world. Behind the speakers' table was a huge map of the United States with a flashing green light showing where Beaver Falls was and a sign that read, "Thanks for putting us on the map." Huge pictures of Joe were mounted all over the field house. The two aisles on the main floor were labeled Broadway and Seventh Avenue to represent the most famous streets in New York and Beaver Falls. And everybody in the world was there, including all the football celebrities from the parade and more than a score of Joe's relatives. Joe's brother, Sonny, looked especially nice in his army dress uniform complete with all of his decorations.

After the meal, the program began with filmed highlights of the Super Bowl. I got nervous all over again watching the game unfold in front of my eyes, but it was just marvelous watching the Jets win a second time.

Then the speeches began. Butch Newton, the president of the Beaver Falls High School Boosters Club, gave a short welcoming speech. You will remember that this is the same Boosters Club which sponsored the special football training camp for about fifty of the most promising junior high athletes Joe's sophomore year, and you'll remember that the Beaver Falls coaches didn't select Joe as one of the sixty. George Sauer gave his speech and Johnny Sample, the defensive captain of the Jets, gave his. Both were short. Then it was Don Maynard's turn and he didn't want to stop. With that Texas twang of his, everybody had a hard time understanding him, but Joe said that when you give Don a free meal he feels obligated to give you your money's worth.

I was next. Clive Rush, a former Jet assistant who had become the head coach of the Boston Patriots, presented me with a nice plaque and then I began. The audience started to chuckle when I shuffled through my notes, but I had chosen my words carefully and had rehearsed them for days. First thing I looked Joe straight in the eye and said, "Sit up straight. Your posture is bad enough without you sliding down in your chair like that."

I thanked everybody who had had anything to do with "Joe Namath Day" and told them how proud I was to have a good son like Joe. I recounted some of Joey's and Linny's adventures—if I had told them all, I would have spoken longer than Don Maynard—and I explained how difficult and hilarious it was to be the mother of five precocious kids. And then I sat down. I wouldn't want to be the one to say it, but people told me it was the best speech of the night.

Other people talked—Phil Iselin, who a year earlier had become president of the Jets, state senator Ernest Kline, Joe Tronzo, the sports editor of the Beaver Falls *News-Tribune*, Bill Ross, and Larry Bruno—and then it was Joe's turn.

With a deadpan look and a twinkle in his eye, Joe opened with a story about a part-time job he'd gotten at Alabama working as the chauffeur for a very attractive lady who lived in a big house in Tuscaloosa.

My ears perked up. I'd never before heard Joe mention such a job.

"One day while I was putting away some groceries for her," Joe said, "the lady called to me from her bedroom. I went up and she said, 'Joseph, take off my dress.' Well, one thing my mother taught me was to always be polite and do what I was told. So I took off her dress."

My God, I thought, what on earth is going on?

"Then the lady said, 'Joseph, take off my slip.'"

I wanted to hide.

"Then she said, 'Joseph, take off my bra.'"

I looked around. People were starting to get nervous.

" . . . My mother told me to always obey, so I took off her bra. Then she asked me to take off her panties, and once again I obeyed. Finally, the lady looked at me and said, 'Joseph, don't ever let me catch you wearing my clothes again.'"

Well, after a nervous second or two, the field house shook with laughter. I sighed a big sigh of relief and burst out laughing, too. I started to realize right then that if Joe could put on his own mother, he could do a pretty good job of putting on other people, too. But let me talk about that in a later chapter.

The rest of the night went smoothly and I could tell Joe was having a great time. At the end of the ceremonies Joe awarded the first annual Joe Namath Scholarship to a Beaver Falls High School football player named Dennis Caldwell. Joe said with a grin, "This scholarship doesn't mean you have to follow in my academic tradition."

After the banquet Joe's friends and his brothers went to another party at the clubhouse of the nearby Blackhawk Golf Course, mainly, I think, because Geneva College doesn't allow liquor to be served anywhere on campus, and more than a few people were getting a little thirsty. I was too. Before long, with the help of a little Johnny Walker Red, I think it was, Joe and his brothers were playing slot-bowling and yelling and cheating on each other, just like they had in the old days. Joe's fame hadn't changed things for him very much at all, at least not around Beaver Falls.

Early the next morning, Joe and his party left for New York, and the young lady with the see-through blouse gave the people of Beaver Falls something else to talk about. This time she was wearing one of those bare-midriff harem suits with see-through *pants.* Some of the guys around town still talk about having another "Joe Namath Day," but I wonder if they're more interested in my son or his traveling companions.

Indeed, Joe could stir up a small storm even at his own party, but not long after all the hullabaloo had quieted down I got to thinking about exactly what it is that makes Joe so controversial. Maybe it's simply what Sonny Werblin said it was: star quality. I see Joe from the rather narrow perspective of being his mother, of course, and maybe I sometimes tend to look the other way when it comes to his faults. But I don't really think so. For sure, Joey was never a little angel all the time, and he isn't now. Who in this world is perfect? On the other hand, every time I pick up a newspaper and find Joe's gotten himself involved in this thing or that, I can't help but think back to the days of his childhood when he was always saying, "Everybody picks on me."

Joe has been criticized for his life-style, for the money he makes, for the people he associates with—in fact, for almost everything under the sun. The more I think about it, the more I feel people just don't take the time to find out what Joe is really like. It's strange, but the people who hate Joe the most are the ones who know him the least. His enemies never bother to find out for themselves what makes Joe tick. Even if they've never had the opportunity to know him personally, it hasn't prevented them from mouthing off or passing false rumors.

I sometimes wish the controversies weren't there, but I do have to admit they sure have made life interesting—his and mine both. The liveliest time of all came in the spring and summer of 1969, not long after he had achieved his greatest success. That's when he tangled with Mr. Pete Rozelle, who was, and is, the commissioner (shall I reveal my prejudice right now and say dictator?) of the National Football League. Their little confrontation almost caused Joe to give up football forever.

The average career of a professional football player, as I've pointed out, is only about five years long—only miracle workers last ten or more—and then it's out into the hard world of business. Joe, like most other ballplayers, looked long and hard for some outside investments that would secure his future. With two longtime friends, Bobby Van and Ray Abbruzzese, he bought a nightclub on New York's swinging Eastside and called it Bachelors III. It was a logical choice. After he'd been in the Big Apple a couple of years, he had become almost as much of an expert on night life as he was on football.

Bachelors III was a good investment. It was a nice place where you could get the best food, have the biggest drinks, and meet your friends, and people came from all over for an evening's entertainment. Everything was going along just fine until one day in the spring of 1969. Pete Rozelle said he was curious about some of the people who frequented Joe's place. He said the commissioner's office had learned that some of the people who went to Bachelors III were members of the underworld, or the mob, or whatever you want to call it. He said that since the standard player's contract stipulates professional football players can't associate with "undesirables," Joe might have to sell his share of Bachelors III before he reported to camp for the 1969 season.

When the news broke, Joe called me and I could tell he was almost crying. He said he really loved football, but that he just couldn't let Pete Rozelle step all over him like that. It was unfair to his partners, Joe said, and it was unfair to him, too. When Joe was in the club, he often went out of his way to talk with his guests, just like any good host would do. Just because some of Joe's guests had last names that ended in a vowel didn't automatically make them members of the mob. And even if they were, Pete Rozelle was saying Joe was guilty by association.

Joe said he would quit the game rather than let Rozelle dictate his life off the field, and I agreed with him 100 percent. I told him he should quit, too.

What was Joe supposed to do? I could understand if he had been operating a gambling house or something like that, but all he was doing was trying to run a respectable nightclub. And besides, how do you spot an "undesirable" in the first place? Do you stand by the door and ask everybody who tries to come in, "Excuse me, sir. Are you by chance a member of the underworld? Oh, you are? Well, then, would you please be so kind as to take your business elsewhere?" Maybe Joe should have put up a sign that said: "No Mobsters Allowed." Do you see the position he was in?

That was only the beginning. Next, the press started working its imagination overtime, as it always seemed to do with Joe. *Life* was the first. It called Bachelors III a "hoodlum-haunted" nightclub (maybe because there were so many press people hanging around there in those days). But the *Life* story did have at least one bit of humor. It said Joe had blue eyes, while of course everybody knows they're a marvelous shade of green.

Newsweek followed with its shot, but didn't seem to add much to what *Life* had said. Then the writers at *Sports Illustrated* came out with a real blast. They said there had been crap games being run out of Joe's apartment all during January and February of 1969. If they had known the true facts, they would have known that Joe wasn't even in New York at the time. In the first part of January, of course, he was in Miami winning the Super Bowl. After that he spent several weeks in Japan, Okinawa, and Hawaii visiting army hospitals. Then he played in a golf tournament in San Diego and, finally, he flew to Fort

Joe Namath burst on the Alabama scene in 1962 as the nation's most celebrated sophomore.

Above—Before he injured his knee, Namath was a sensational runner as well as passer. Right—Tuscaloosa businessman Jack Warner was an early friend of Joe and his mother Rose.

Alabama Coach Paul "Bear" Bryant knew he had something special the first time he saw Joe Namath practice.

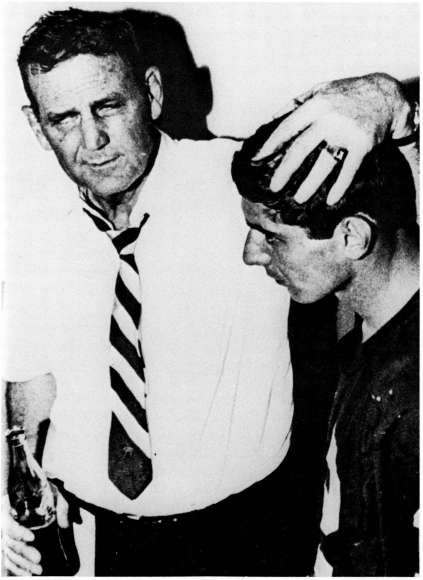

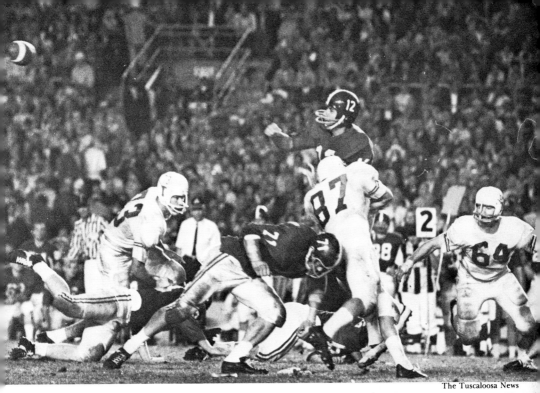

The Tuscaloosa News

Opposite page: Coach "Bear" Bryant walks dejectedly off the field after Namath injures a knee that is to haunt him.

Above—Namath stands in the pocket against a heavy rush and burns a forward pass in his record performance against Texas in the Orange Bowl. Right—"The man with the Golden Horn," Al Hirt, joins Joe and members of the Alabama team for a gag shot in Paul Bryant Hall.

The Tuscaloosa News

Above—Namath dives for vital yardage in his last game against arch-rival Auburn. Right—Namath leaps high in the air and fires a completion against Georgia Tech.

Victor Mikus

His college career behind him, Namath signs a $427,000 contract; in his shades and fur coat he becomes "Broadway Joe" of the New York Jets.

Opposite page: Top— Namath hits the heights as a professional, leading the Jets to the Super Bowl Championship. On his right is Jet Coach Weeb Eubank. Bottom—Coach Eubank and Namath go over their strategy during the Super Bowl in Miami.

Right—It's autograph time for Joe anytime a fan can reach him. Below—Joe's "cup runneth over" with victory after the Super Bowl.

Victor Mikus

Studio 41

Beaver Falls News-Tribune

Beaver Falls News-Tribune

Top—Beaver Falls has a "Joe Namath Day" to salute hometown-boy-made-good. Above—The little Pennsylvania city all but shut down to celebrate Joe's homecoming.

Opposite page: Top—Despite personal injuries and a decline in the Jets, Namath keeps standing in the pocket and winging his passes, as in this game with Washington. Bottom—Joe is helped off the field after another knee injury. This painful scene had begun to dominate his career.

Studio 41

Studio 41

John Zimmerman TIME-LIFE Picture Agency © Time Inc.

Opposite page: Joe continues to bounce back after his injuries and remains one of the most popular sports stars in America.

Namath, typically, has his own answer to the snowflakes as he warms up for a home game in New York.

Top—The Namath children gather to celebrate Mama's book: (L-R) John, Bobby, Rose, Joe, Rita, and Franklin. Above left—Joe relaxes between scenes of one of three movies he has appeared in. Above right—Singer Jimmy Dean and Rose help Joe open one of his restaurants.

Opposite page: Joe and Rose stand in front of the "Wall of Fame" his mother has assembled during his career.

Joe Namath in 1975 turned down a $4 million offer to join the World Football League. Despite his injuries he remains one of pro football's all-time great quarterbacks.

Lauderdale, Florida, where he lives most of the winter. The
story was ridiculous and blatantly untrue, but I guess it sold a
lot of magazines.

As if the crazy magazine stories weren't bad enough, the
good old-fashioned rumor mill switched into high gear. One
said that Joe's threatening to quit was just a publicity stunt, but
if there's one thing Joe has never needed it's fabricated
publicity. He's always generated plenty by just taking a deep
breath. Another story making the rounds said Joe didn't want
to play football anymore, because his legs hurt too much. Well,
Joe's legs hurt through most of his senior year at Alabama and
through four years with the Jets, and if he had wanted out of
pro football because of bad legs, he never would have gotten in.

The wildest rumor of all, though, was that Joe was about to
be kicked out of the league for throwing two games during the
championship season of 1968—the ones against Buffalo and
Denver in which he had thrown five interceptions each. Now,
even I know that if a quarterback wants to throw a football
game or even shade the points a little he's not going to do it by
throwing interceptions. That's just too obvious. What he is
going to do are little, inconspicuous things like handing off the
ball too high or too late to a running back or calling the wrong
kind of play to make it look like somebody else is messing up.
Joe said in his own book he tried to throw the Super Bowl by
handing off wrong to Matt Snell and by throwing wobbly passes
to receivers like Don Maynard and George Sauer. But—in the
official Joe Willie Namath put-on—Joe said those guys just
wouldn't cooperate. Matt Snell ran for over a hundred yards
and Don Maynard and George Sauer kept making impossible
catches all afternoon.

Still, the reporters kept writing up the rumors and all the
other nonsense, and I think that for a while a lot of people even
fell for it. No wonder Joe doesn't like certain members of the
press very much.

It turned out a lot of pretty influential people didn't want Joe
to retire. NBC television, which had the rights to the American
Football Conference games—remember, in two seasons the
merger between the two leagues would be complete—wasn't
too happy about Joe's impending absence. Nor were Jets season
ticket holders. Nor were the owners of the Baltimore Colts, the
Cleveland Browns, and the Pittsburgh Steelers, the three teams

which had only recently switched to the AFC under terms of the merger. (I never have figured that one out. If Joe kept on playing, those teams would just have to get more used to losing.) Joe meant big box office for several parties, and it was obvious that money talks.

All of a sudden everybody was up against the wall. Pete Rozelle couldn't back down because it would have loosened his dictatorial hold on the game, and Joe wouldn't back down because he refused to be disloyal to his friends and business partners. But Joe also realized he owed loyalty to his teammates, the guys who had struggled so long with him to reach the top. Joe was being torn up more by this dilemma than by anything else.

In late June, Joe, Jimmy Walsh, and Weeb Ewbank held a meeting with Rozelle. Rozelle said he understood Joe's position and even admitted Joe hadn't done anything wrong himself. But Rozelle was adamant and nothing was settled.

Joe didn't report to training camp on time. He couldn't, because the whole issue was still up in the air when preseason practice began. However, he did meet with his teammates to try and explain what was happening. Afterward one of his teammates said, "Hey, Joe. When the commissioner finds out I've been associating with an undesirable like you and kicks me out of football, can you get me a job with the mob?"

Finally, on July 13, Jimmy Walsh proposed a compromise to Rozelle. Joe would sell his interest in Bachelors III, but he could enter into another partnership with Bobby Van and Ray Abbruzzese any time and any place he wanted. The three of them could open another restaurant next door the next day if they chose. Joe still didn't feel completely right about the deal, but in the end he went along. Joe had to bend a little, but he hadn't sold out his principles. That was the important thing.

All's well that ends well, because the publicity boosted the popularity of Bachelors III tremendously. Eventually, even more Bachelor IIIs were opened in other cities around the country.

As for Rozelle, I think my son could have stuck it to him pretty good if he had wanted to, but the nice guy in Joe just wouldn't let him do it. Rozelle is still the commissioner, but he seems to be spending more and more time these days in courtrooms all over the country trying to defend the methods the NFL establishment uses to keep control over its players. He has other responsibilities too, of course. He has to throw out the first football of the season and give the awards after every Super Bowl, but so far he seems to be holding up well under the pressure.

Oh, I should be fairer to Rozelle than that, I guess. Professional football seems to be the only game in town these days, and the way he packaged and promoted the sport had a lot to do with the tremendous boom it enjoyed in the 1960s. But don't think promoting the game is as tough as playing it.

The Bachelors III incident was by far the most dramatic bit of controversy in Joe's public life, but it sure wasn't the first. Even in high school there were all sorts of absurd rumors about him. Joe Tronzo, the sports editor of the Beaver Falls *News-Tribune*, wrote a hilarious column about my son not too long after his last high school football game.

"There are stories that Joe Namath sawed a cow in half in the high school auditorium," Tronzo wrote, "that he punched a pregnant woman; that he tried to bomb a school board member's house; that he poured gasoline on a fifth grader and lit the kid; that he threw eggs at [vice-president] Nixon. And that the only thing he passed at B.F.H.S. was a football."

To be sure, Joe didn't get along with a lot of his teachers, and I think his football coach, Larry Bruno, must have spent as much time trying to smooth out the ruffled feathers of high school administrators as he did running his football team. Part of the trouble, I must admit, was that Joe was a lazy student. However, a lot of people at the high school were just plain jealous of all the ink the football team got—and, of course, Joe was the star of the football team.

At Alabama the whole process repeated itself. Right from the beginning, false rumors started up about Joe. The first time he got national attention was when Coach Bryant suspended him near the end of his junior year for breaking training rules. But from the first day he stepped on campus with that toothpick dangling from his mouth and climbed the practice field tower to say "Hi" to Coach Bryant, not only his teammates but the whole city of Tuscaloosa and maybe even the entire state of Alabama was buzzing about this Yankee boy from the steel mill country of western Pennsylvania.

What was the image and what was the reality? From the rumor mill you'd have thought Joe was a cross between Errol Flynn and Burt Reynolds or guys like that, but let me turn a section of this chapter over to a couple of Joe's Alabama teammates who have been his good friends now for over ten years. Maybe they can shed a little light on what the real Joe Namath was like, then and now. One is Gaylon McCollough, whom I mentioned earlier. Gaylon was perhaps closer to Joe than anybody, being Joe's center from their freshman year on—but he isn't exactly your stereotyped jock, either. Right now he's a very successful cosmetic surgeon in Birmingham, Alabama. The other player is Curtis Crenshaw, who was three years ahead of Joe but got to know him well a little bit later through mutual friends like Ray Abbruzzese and Jimmy Walsh. Today Curtis is a certified public accountant and a co-owner of a Birmingham architectural firm.

McCollough: "I can remember all through school hearing those horrible stories about what Joe was doing at the University. I come from a small town in Alabama—Thomasville—and whenever I'd go home people were always asking about Joe, asking if those stories were true. There was a black girl enrolled at school—one of the first blacks ever to attend Alabama—and there were all sorts of rumors that she and Joe were going out together. I knew better than that. And in his junior year, when we lost to Auburn, 10–8, Joe's performance was not the best, nor was anybody's performance very good that day. It was a windy, miserable afternoon and I think Joe was something like three for seventeen. But immediately the story was out that Joe had spent the night before the game in jail because of drinking. There were always stories like that going around, and they always made me very upset because you shouldn't have had to defend anybody who was as devoted to a football team, and to himself, as Joe was.

"Some people just have public magnetism. And other people just like to talk about the ones who do, I guess, because in certain circles, if you tell an exciting story about a prominent individual, you find that people listen. Pretty soon you wind up fabricating stories because then you learn people listen even more. I know Joe was aware of these stories, and I'm sure it hurt him to know people were thinking these sort of things about him because Joe wasn't like that. Not at all."

Crenshaw: "Possibly the only thing you could call flashy about Joe Namath was his dress. When he first came to Alabama he didn't have a big wardrobe, but what he did have

was pretty wild. And of course his play on the football field *was*
flashy. But his private life was very simple, I think. He didn't
date a lot. He did go out with the roommate of Gaylon's future
wife a couple of times, but he certainly didn't have the playboy
image he later gained notoriety and fame for. I found him to be
a very sincere person. We've known each other for more than
ten years now, and I still think he's the same rather basic,
simple, down-to-earth person he was at Alabama. He was
always glad to see his friends and his family—he was very close
to both his mother and father even though they had separated—and when his brothers came down to see him it was always
a visit he looked forward to.

"I went to New York on a business trip shortly after he was
named Rookie of the Year in the AFL. I tried to get in touch
with him but the Jets' front office wouldn't give me his number.
Finally, one of the secretaries said she'd call Joe and ask him to
call me. He did, and went out of his way for a week to make
sure I saw the city properly and had things to do. He didn't
have to do that. He could have just said, 'It's nice to have you in
New York and I hope you have a good time,' and I would never
have felt anything bad about that at all. But he went out of his
way because that's the kind of guy he really is."

McCollough: "Even today the public image of Joe disturbs
me because it's just not the person Curtis and I know; it's not
the same person the average man in the street thinks he knows.
If you mention his name to people and they say they don't like
him, never did like him, and you ask them why, you find out it's
because of what they've seen about him on television or
something like that. But that's a different image from the way
the man really is. He's a professional, not only as a pro athlete
but as an entertainer as well, what with all his commercials and
movies. I think Joe goes along with this image sometimes
because that's what's expected of him. Also, he has an absolutely great sense of humor. Sometimes I get the impression people
don't realize when he's working his official Joe Namath put-on,
which he does a lot."

Crenshaw: "Sometimes I've seen this happen: I'll be with
some people who want to meet Joe, then they finally meet
him—and immediately come out with some statement to try
and antagonize him, just to see what his reaction will be. Then
they go away and say, 'We don't like him. We didn't think we'd

like him and we don't.' It's almost like when you go to a movie you've made up your mind not to like and then wind up not liking it. Very few people, I think, approach Joe with an open mind. Maybe that's impossible because of all the preconceived notions about him they're bound to get from the media."

McCollough: "But Joe never looked for a fistfight with these kind of people, although there were a lot of times when he would have been more than justified. If somebody said something he didn't like, he'd try and drop the conversation. He tried to keep good team morale and good team spirit, because he was interested in winning more than anything else.

"You know? My nine-year-old son loves Joe Namath. He's heard me talk about Joe; he knows I played football with him and he's very proud of that fact. Well, he came home from school one day and said his class was going to put on a little play and that all of his classmates had to dress up as famous people.

" 'Who are you going to be?' I asked.

" 'Joe Namath.'

" 'Who's going to be me?'

" 'Daddy, nobody's going to be you. They don't know who you are.' "

But Gaylon McCollough can rest assured Joe Namath knows who he is. He doesn't forget his friends, not ever.

In the pros, it wasn't so much the rumors that caused the controversies—with the notable exception of what happened during the Bachelors III episode—as it was the money he was making and the way he spent it, which should have been nobody's business but Joe's. The press saw it otherwise, however, and managed to find fault with Joe every time he turned around.

Right after he signed that first $427,000 contract, certain sportswriters wrote, "With his bad knees, Joe Namath isn't worth $4.27." Little things like that. They didn't like it when he bought a mink coat. They didn't like it when he grew his Fu Manchu mustache and they didn't like it when he shaved it off for $10,000. They didn't even like it when he decorated his New York apartment with lush, white rugs. I never did figure out what interior decorating had to do with throwing a football.

Then there was the criticism from other players around the league. Frank Ryan, who was the quarterback for the Cleveland Browns when Joe was a rookie with the Jets, said flat out that if

Joe was worth $400,000, he was worth $1 million. Well, maybe that's the kind of thinking you do when you're a doctor of mathematics, which Frank is, but I always felt in my own mind the good Dr. Ryan was a mathematician first and a quarterback second. Joe's never going to be a mathematician like the good doctor. All he can do is throw touchdown passes. And the score in Super Bowl victories when Frank retired was Namath 1, Ryan 0. Even Joe and I can understand that kind of arithmetic.

As the years went by, some of the attacks got pretty personal. Shortly after the Jets' Super Bowl victory, Earl Morrall (you remember Earl: he's the former quarterback for the Baltimore Colts who is now with the Miami Dolphins) said he never wanted any of his kids to grow up to be like Joe Namath. Now that was serious, because what Earl had intended as a criticism of Joe was also a direct slap at me. After all, I was Joe's mother and had raised him to the best of my ability. Attack my son and you attack me. I thought I had done a pretty good job with Joe, but when Earl made that remark, I didn't know what to think and I was very hurt.

But I finally realized that, as far as I could tell, what motivated Earl to say what he had said was nothing more than petty jealousy. Suddenly I felt a whole lot better about Joe and me. For Earl, though, I felt only pity because jealousy can be a destructive thing.

Earl is right about one thing. Kids are real hero-worshipers, and I think it's important for youngsters to have people they can look up to. I sure remember my hero: Spencer Tracy. I loved him both as an actor and as a man.

When Joey was a little boy, his hero was another quarterback from western Pennsylvania who made it pretty big in the pros, a guy by the name of Johnny Unitas. The year Joe entered high school was the year Johnny U. led the Baltimore Colts to their tremendous overtime victory over the New York Giants for the National Football League championship. When Joe was a star in high school, his teammates started calling him "Joey U." and he loved it. Even today, Joe speaks of Unitas with the greatest respect.

So Joe knows the importance of the athlete-as-hero. For that very reason he has always tried to conduct himself carefully both on and off the field. He knows there are a lot of young boys out there dreaming about the day when they will lead their team to the Super Bowl, just like Joe used to dream about being Johnny U. in that championship game of 1958.

So in the end, that's why I was upset about what Morrall had said about Joe. It wasn't because he had criticized Joe—I know my own son—but because he wasn't setting a very good example by revealing how jealous he was of Joe's success.

Besides, Morrall's kids could do worse than to grow up to be like Joe. My gosh. They could be rich, famous, and successful, and maybe even win the Super Bowl.

I don't want to be too hard on Earl. After all, he was the NFL's Most Valuable Player in 1968, and despite his poor performance in that season's Super Bowl, he did come back two years later to help the Colts win Super Bowl V. And that isn't all bad.

A lot of Joe's problems, I think, have been caused by the press and its unending search for sensationalism. Joe doesn't mind criticism of himself as a football player—he's his own worst critic, in fact. I just wish sportswriters would be willing to write about Joe as a football player and give him some peace and quiet in his private life—or at the very least, let him present his side of a controversy.

Joe's been antagonistic towards the press for a long time—not towards all its members, of course, just the ones he considers to be unfair and inaccurate. Like the ones who write that he's got blue eyes when they're really green, or that Beaver Falls is a coal mining town when it's really a steel mill town. Small things like that, and bigger ones, too.

I remember Joe's first press conference after he signed with the New York Jets. One writer had to ask the traditional question: Did Joe take basket weaving at Alabama?

Joe looked him right in the eye and said, "Naaw. That was too hard. I took journalism instead."

That wasn't exactly a tactful statement, but Joe knew the press—especially the New York press—had it in for him even before he put on a Jets' uniform and he wasn't about to let them get the upper hand.

Joe does have good friends in the press, however, those writers and broadcasters who report without prejudice, take the time to find out what he's really like, and let him give his side of a story. His two favorites of all time, I think, are Dave

Anderson, the columnist for *The New York Times,* and Howard
Cosell, the radio and television personality.

Joe likes Dave Anderson because he goes to a lot of trouble to get his facts right. If, for example, Joe throws an interception, he doesn't just assume that Joe made an error. He knows the interception might have been caused by a receiver who ran the wrong pattern, by a lineman who missed a blocking assignment, or by a defensive halfback who simply made a great play. Dave doesn't rush to conclusions, and he's careful. Joe appreciates that.

And he likes Howard Cosell because . . . oh heck, doesn't everybody like Howard? I know I do. I don't admire him because he says nice things about Joe as much as I do because he's a man who says what he believes. When Howard likes something, he'll tell you, and when he doesn't like something, he'll tell you that, too, and why. When Howard Cosell speaks, you know you can believe what he's saying—even though this paragon of virtue, this man of quality, this authoritative walking thesaurus of knowledge uses a lot of big words I sometimes can't understand.

I remember seeing him once on a television show when he was asked: "Who is the greatest professional football player in America?"

Without any hesitation Howard answered, "Joe Willie Namath is the greatest."

When a man says something like that about your very own son, you've just got to love him. Right?

Being the mother of a celebrity isn't always easy. Mostly it's been a lot of fun, especially in recent years, and I've always stood a little straighter when I've heard people say, "There goes Joe Namath's mother." But let me tell you, there have been some times.

In 1968 Joe made his first movie, a light comedy called "Norwood." That was okay. In 1970 he made "The Last Rebel," a post-Civil War western. That was okay, too. In 1969, however, he made a third movie with Ann-Margret called "C. C. Rider & Co.," and right away the talk around Beaver Falls was that Joe had made a dirty movie. I didn't believe it; I knew Joe would never do something like that. But I must admit I was curious, and when it came to western Pennsylvania I decided to see for myself. Of course, I didn't dare go see it in Beaver Falls. This was shortly after the time Earl Morrall and the others were spouting off about the bad example Joe was setting for American youth. On the outside chance "C. C. Rider & Co." did turn out to be a little risque, I didn't want to give the folks in Beaver Falls anything more to talk about. I could just hear them whispering: "Joe Namath makes dirty movies and his mother goes to *see* them."

So Aunt Anna—the same one I'd played cards with during

the *Heidi* Bowl—and I went over to Rochester, Pennsylvania,
one afternoon to see what the fuss was all about.

It was nice and dark and nobody recognized us as we took
two seats way in the back of the huge theater. The only problem
was that our seats were broken. If we sat tilted to the right,
everything was fine. But if we tried to sit up straight, the seats
tipped forward and tended to dump us on the floor, which
turned out to be very handy.

For the first few minutes of the movie there wasn't any
problem. I knew all those people had been wrong about Joe
just like they usually were.

Then it happened. Joe and Ann-Margret got into bed. Oh
Lord, I thought, as we both sat bolt upright—and almost slid
under the seats in front of us as our own seats gave way. All I
could see were a couple of pairs of legs waving back and forth
on the screen. By the time Aunt Anna and I got straightened
out, Joe and Ann-Margret were out of bed and the film
continued.

This happened all afternoon. Joe and Ann-Margret would
get into bed, and Aunt Anna and I would sit up straight, slide
to the floor, and see nothing but those legs flapping about. By
the end of the film I couldn't really have told you whether it was
a dirty movie or not. But I somehow suspected it was.

That night on the telephone I told Joe I thought it was wrong
for him to be in a movie that was even a little bit suggestive.

"Oh, Mom," Joe said, with what I thought was a trace of
exasperation, "nothing happened. After all, we both wore pink
tights and we didn't ever really do anything."

But he agreed with me about making dirty movies. I was
right and he knew it. He promised to be more selective in the
future about his off-the-field activities. Why, he even went so
far as to turn down a lot of money to appear in the centerfold
of one of those new nudie pinup magazines. Thank goodness. I
could just imagine what poor Earl Morrall would have said if
Joe had ever done that.

Then there was the time Joe gave me a new car, a Dodge
Charger he had been awarded as the most valuable player in
the 1969 Super Bowl. He left it parked in front of my house the
morning after that "Joe Namath Day" celebration in Beaver
Falls. I thought the gift was very nice of Joe—he's always been
generous towards me and the rest of his family since he started

to make some money—but there was only one problem. I didn't know how to drive. Although I was fifty-four years old at the time, I honestly had never been behind the wheel of a car in my life. I didn't know the difference between a steering wheel and a hubcap.

"No problem," said Franklin, who just happened to be around. "We'll get a learner's permit and I'll teach you myself."

Okay, I thought. No reason to worry. Franklin says there's nothing to it.

A few days later I was ready.

"Put the car in P for park and turn the key," said Franklin, after securely fastening his seat belt.

"That was easy," I said, as the big engine roared to life. I didn't realize the Dodge Charger that year was practically a racing car.

"Now all you do is move the gear shift into D for drive," Franklin continued, tightening his shoulder harness. "That way you'll go forward when you step on the gas."

I stepped and we went, and the next thing I knew we were leaving rubber all over Fourth Avenue. I jumped a curb. Franklin yelled for me to hit the brakes. I would have been delighted. I didn't know where they were. We continued down the sidewalk at an alarming rate of speed.

"The brakes! The brakes!" Franklin shouted, and Franklin never shouts at his mother.

Somehow—I don't remember exactly how—the car stopped without hitting anything big and Franklin, shaking and mumbling, drove me home.

I never did go to a driving school, which I probably should have done. Many friends and many lessons later, though, I earned my license and was ready to solo. This time around I was more careful. I had gained a lot of respect for that monster. I made it to the grocery store and did my shopping. On the way back to the car I ran into Whitey Harris, who'd been a halfback on the Beaver Falls High School football team Joe's senior year.

"Sure is a nice looking car," Whitey said, sticking his head inside the passenger-side window.

"Sure is, Whitey," I said. "It's the one Joe got at the Super Bowl."

I started up, carefully moving the gearshift from P to D with my foot on the brake.

"Wow, just listen to that cam," Whitey said. "And look at all that power equipment."

I didn't want Whitey to think I didn't know what a cam was—still don't—so I launched into an explanation of the various accessories, all the while merrily pushing buttons in and out.

Suddenly I heard a gagging sound from the other side of the car. I turned and discovered I'd power-equipped the passenger window right up under poor Whitey's chin.

Poor Whitey started choking and I started getting excited. I accidentally slipped my foot off the brake and all three of us—Whitey, the car, and me—jerked forward. This time, however, I *did* know where the brakes were. I applied them forcefully. And rolled down the window.

Whitey backed away from the car with a strange look on his face (I think it was fear) and began running. Even to this day whenever Whitey sees me coming, I see him going. I don't understand. All the other people in Beaver Falls are very interested in my driving. They even pull off to the side of the road and watch.

What I don't have to put up with. Another time Joe gave me and Aunt Anna a trip to the Hawaiian Islands for a vacation present. Jimmy Walsh's mother, Elsie, went with us, too. We had a fine old time running around and getting tan and in general acting like three college kids at Fort Lauderdale. Just how fine a time we'd had became apparent when the hotel manager called Aunt Anna and me into his office and said, "Ladies, you have just run your bill to over $3,000. Will you be paying by cash or credit card?"

"Well, uh," I stammered, "my son will pay for it. I'm sure he's made the proper arrangements."

Which, in fact, is usually what happens. Joe or Jimmy Walsh just calls up and sets things, so all I have to do is sign the tab. It's really great, except this time around there had been a mix-up.

"No one has made the arrangements, as you choose to call them," the manager said arrogantly. "Now how do you plan to settle the account?"

"I'm *sure* the arrangements have been made. My *son* will *pay* for it."

Now I was getting a little arrogant and a little hot under the collar, too.

"If you can't keep your records straight," I continued, "it's not my fault."

"Just who is your son?"

"Joe Namath."

"Joe Namath? Well, I see, Mrs. Namath. Could you please show me some identification?"

I took out my driver's license. He stared at it for a long time. Finally he said, "Everything is perfectly clear, Rose. Except in the Islands we don't very often spell Namath 'S-z-o-l-n-o-k-i.' "

It took a few long-distance calls to Mr. Walsh back in New York to get that one straightened out.

Being the mother of a pretty famous guy caught up with me again on that very same trip. One afternoon Aunt Anna and I went on a hike with some friends we'd met. The day started out in glorious sunshine, but in the late afternoon we all got caught in a terrible thunderstorm and arrived back in Honolulu absolutely soaked. No problem. One of our party knew Don Ho, the singer, and we all went over to his club to dry out.

Don took us in like long-lost relatives. He gave us the run of his office, and when we'd recovered a little, he invited us to his night club to see his act. I really didn't want to go considering all I was wearing was a pair of shorts, tennis shoes, and a blouse. Not exactly your standard nightclub getup, even in Hawaii. Besides, my hair was a mess. But Don assured us we'd be seated in a corner where nobody could see me.

So we sort of sneaked in and watched his show. It was super, with a big spotlight following his every move across the huge stage.

Don finished the first part of his act and took the microphone in his hand. "Good evening, ladies and gentlemen," he said, "and welcome to Don Ho's. Tonight, I have a special surprise for you. Right here, watching our show and gracing my nightclub with her beauty and charm, is Joe Namath's mother. My friend and yours—Rose!"

Then that big spotlight wheeled around and hit me dead in the face. I had absolutely no place to go.

"Come on, Rose," Don smiled. "Stand up so the people can see you."

There was nothing else I could do, although I looked as if I had just crawled out from the pineapple fields.

And I'll bet you thought being the mother of a star was all fun and games.

Most of the time I don't really care one way or the other about being identified as Joe's mother, but there was one afternoon in particular when I was mighty thankful for the association. For the opening game of the 1972 season, about fifty people from Beaver Falls, including my husband Steve and my sons Bobby and Franklin, chartered a bus and drove to Buffalo for the game between the Bills and the Jets. We went up on a Saturday and spent the evening chatting with Joe and his teammates. Late the next morning the bus took us out to War Memorial Stadium for the game. I was just about to take my seat when John Free, the business manager and traveling secretary for the Jets, asked Steve and me if we'd like to watch the game from the press box. It was a cold, blustery day, and we were more than happy to take him up on the offer. Bobby and Franklin remained in the stands.

It was a great afternoon—the Jets won, 41–24—and after the game Steve and I headed off to meet up with my sons. I was glad Steve was with me. I didn't know the main entrance from the team entrance or even the grounds keeper's entrance. But I was sure Steve knew his way around.

Or did he?

I know it's pretty hard to get lost inside a football stadium, but we managed. It took a long time for Bobby and Franklin and some of their friends to track us down. In the meantime, the bus driver had understandably given up on us and headed back to the motel, which was about ten minutes away by car and forty-five minutes by foot. I couldn't see any cabs, and so there we were, all six or seven of us, stranded in the middle of downtown Buffalo. We had no choice but to start walking.

After a while, Bobby and Franklin wandered up a side street in search of a telephone. Just as they disappeared around a corner I spotted a police paddy wagon ambling along. I ran into the middle of the street and flagged it down. "I'm Joe Namath's mother," I announced. "We got separated from our party. Can you get us back to our hotel?"

"Sure you are, lady," said the officer. "And I'm his brother. Move off the street. We haven't got time for nuts like you."

"Now look here, officer. I *am* Joe's mother and I *would* appreciate your help."

After a long discussion they reluctantly believed me. (They must have been Buffalo fans.) Steve and I and the others got in the paddy wagon and started out in search of Bobby and

Franklin. We found them and they just couldn't believe their eyes. Neither could Joe a half-hour later when two paddy wagons—one wasn't enough to hold everybody—pulled up in front of the hotel and unceremoniously deposited his exhausted relatives in the lobby.

Visiting Joe in New York City has been the most fun, I think. At least it has been for me; I'm not sure how Joe feels about it after a couple of escapades I can think of.

On one trip, I decided to run down to Camden, New Jersey, to visit my daughter Rita. Joe made all the arrangements, as usual, and the next morning one of those $20-a-mile limousines pulled up at the door of Joe's Eastside apartment building, and we were off.

"Camden, New Jersey, please," I said firmly. "I'll give you the address when we get there."

"But lady, I thought we were only going to . . . "

"Never mind, young man. My daughter lives in New Jersey. Let's get going."

I called Joe from Rita's house to let him know I'd arrived safely. When he asked about the bus ride, I knew something was wrong.

"But Joe," I stuttered. "You sent the limousine."

"I sent the limousine," Joe said with remarkable restraint, "to take you to the bus station. Camden must be ninety miles away."

In the background I could hear Joe's friends laughing. Joe finally thought it was funny, too, I think. "Hey, fellas," he said. "Guess what my mother's done now?"

Joe tries to get back at me every now and again, though. I vividly remember one night when Joe took me to dinner at one of those fancy restaurants with waiters running around all dressed up in tuxedos and he said, "Stay cool, Mom. But when you get a chance, look around at that gal behind you in the red dress."

I casually dropped my fork to give me an excuse to turn my head, but just as quickly a waiter bounced over and gave me a clean one.

The next time I just turned my head around slowly. "Oh my God, Joe," I shouted. "She isn't wearing anything on top."

Now everybody in the restaurant turned around and looked at Joe and me—while poor Joe turned the color of that lady's

dress, what there was of it. Maybe I wasn't as cool as I thought I
was.

A few days later Joe made arrangements for Aunt Anna and me to have dinner at a Hungarian restaurant not too far from Joe's place. Joe had other plans, but when Aunt Anna and I arrived, I knew we were in for a good time. And it was a good time. The food was marvelous, the wine was plentiful, and the music brought back a lot of memories of life with my Hungarian friends and relatives. Too soon, it seemed, the restaurant closed—for everyone except Aunt Anna and me and the owner and the musicians. The more we danced, the more we drank; and the more we drank, the more we danced. I didn't want it to ever end. On the way back to Joe's apartment we even got the cab driver to sing Hungarian folk songs with us.

It was about four o'clock in the morning when we tiptoed to the door of Joe's apartment. We tried to be quiet, but for some reason we had trouble fitting the key into the lock. Finally the door opened, and there stood Joe with several of his highly amused friends.

"Where have you been?" he laughed. "*We've* been home for three hours, and we tried to keep it quiet because we thought you and Aunt Anna were in the bedroom asleep."

I had a hard time explaining that one. Joe still probably thinks I'm more of a swinger than he is.

Something special—or at least unusual—always seems to happen to me in New York. One Sunday morning I wanted to attend Mass. I got my rosary beads and Aunt Anna, who always seems to be a partner in my adventures although she's the most sedate person you'd ever want to meet, and we went to a nice church around the corner from Joe's place.

I blessed myself and started to say the Rosary when I noticed people staring at me.

I paid no attention and continued on, but after a few minutes Aunt Anna said, "You know, Rose? I don't think this is a Catholic church."

She was right, but it was a nice church and we stayed for the services anyhow. Only I never did get those kneeling and standing parts straight. Someday, though, I think I'll go back and say hello to all those nice Episcopalians.

Part of my responsibility as Joe's mother is to work part-time as his secretary. When he started out in professional football, I was hired to answer his fan mail. Joe wanted to do it himself but he just couldn't keep up, especially during the football season when he often received as many as 500 pieces of mail a day. The post office needed one truck just to haul Joe's mail alone.

Let me tell you, those letters were a real education, and they still are. They come from all parts of the country—big cities, little cities, farm communities, the East Coast, the West Coast, and everywhere in between. And they come from men and women, adults and teen-agers, school kids and kids who aren't even in school yet. Most of them are requests for autographed pictures, and those are always honored. Some are more personal. All of them are interesting, like this one from the parents of a little girl who may be Joe's youngest admirer in the whole country:

> Dear Joe,
>
> We have a little daughter who has had a terrible crush on you since she was old enough to find your pictures in magazines. When we first noticed her attraction for you, she was about fifteen months old, I think.
>
> She will be three next month and this adoration is greater now than ever before. She plays football with her dad and always has to be Joe Namath. She has one pair of shoes which are named after you too; they are her very special Joe Namath shoes. She twitters, giggles, hides her face, and shows a lot of coyness when you're on TV and is very happy when *you* win a ball game. The rest of the team has nothing to do with the win.
>
> We would like a picture of you, Joe, in uniform or out—even both ways.
>
> And if you ever have reason to come to ———we would be very happy to have you visit us.
>
> Thank you, your fans,

That's sort of cute, I think. But other letters often want to make you cry, like this one:

> Dear Joe Namath, How are you?
>
> I am fine but there's one problem. I cannot walk. I'm crippled. And I sent you this letter because I wanted to have your autograph and a picture of you and a football and uniform for my brother Bobby. His size is size 12

and his helmet size is 7$\frac{1}{2}$, so please send me the
uniform so I could give it to my brother for his birthday.

Love,

There are a lot of letter writers who understand about Joe's knees, because they've got problems of their own that make Joe's pale by comparison:

Mr. Namath,

Before you write this letter off to the trash can, please let me explain. You are the best person I could think of to ask this question. The subject is "knees" on "knees."

I have just had my ninth operation on my right knee, from a simple football knee to the removal of my kneecap. This may seem small to you after all you've been through, but I thought you may understand. I have been the whole route from exercises, shots, Lenox Hill braces to operations. My question is—How do you keep *going*!! I'm ready to give up. Maybe you won't understand, but I don't know where to go. No one else can understand the stress I am going through. Everyone keeps saying, "Slow down. Needlepoint is a lot of fun!" But I'm a woman of twenty-one and I'm not ready for Saturday sports on television.

Maybe you think this letter is crazy, but my only expression for you is fantastic. I cannot believe you are still so active. You never seem depressed or put out by your knees or let them get you down. If you have a secret you would like to share, I would really appreciate knowing it.

Godspeed,

Well, how do you begin to answer a letter like that? Joe doesn't have any secrets about how he deals with his knees. What kind of secret can there be for living with continual pain? It's humbling, though, to realize that no matter how bad off you may think you are, there's always somebody who's got it worse.

One letter came from a little boy in Niles, Ohio, named Brian Cimanero. He was suffering from a rare disease, and to save his life, the doctors had to amputate parts of his fingers and legs. Brian had the dream of meeting Joe Namath, and for some reason I decided to arrange this. When I called Brian and told him I was Joe's mother, he couldn't believe it—and he really had a hard time believing it when I told him we were going to New York to meet Joe. Well, for Brian, it all came true and he did meet Joe. In fact, Joe was Brian's godfather for his confirmation. And believe me, there are plenty of other stories like this in Joe's life, but people never hear about them or read about them.

Sometimes the letters are a little far out, like this one from a girl in the Southwest:

Dear Joe Namath,

If I may be so audacious as to address you by your first name, this is the fourth attempt I've made toward writing a letter to you. Each letter would state the sincerity of the content, but in reading each of them over, I realized how insincere and deceitful each was. Now I shall be totally honest with you. I wanted to write a very cute and interesting short letter; something which would strike your attention and single out my letter from all the others you no doubt must receive from strangers.

Joe, I am a twenty-four-year-old college senior in complete possession of my faculties, and as a new fan of yours, wish to make a request. No doubt my next line will be a real shocker, but if you've read this far, please continue. Joe Namath, will you please call me so that I may speak to you in person? The one wonderful thing which I want very much is a chance to talk to you. You have become my idol and I would like to ask you so many questions about your life that I could never write them all in a letter. Joe, I promise not to say things like, "I love you." I only want to ask you questions about the way you think and feel about different things. If you grant me this wish I shall be the happiest person in the world. I am not dying, but this request is as serious and honest as a person's last wish. Joe, if I have insulted you or angered you by this request, please forgive me and know I shall never bother you again. I realize you must be a very busy man. On the other hand, if you will do this, please call at the designated time below. I will pay the charges.

Sincerely,

Occasionally a letter comes addressed to me in the hope I might indulge in a little influence peddling:

Dear Mrs. Namath:

I know you will forward this letter to your handsome son because you understand a mother's love. I have this nineteen-year-old daughter who is just wonderful. I could never see her marrying anyone except Joe, so I have been saving her for your son. My daughter's measurements are 36-22-36. She has blonde hair, blue eyes and stands five feet, four inches. Most of the other fellows in the neighborhood say she is really a great girl and I know that Joe would be happy with her. Understand I only want the best for my daughter. She could make Joe very happy.

Sincerely,

Couldn't you just see me taking that letter to Joe and saying, "Honey, she sounds like a nice enough girl to me. Why not give it a try and marry her?"

One very strange letter came enclosed with a stick of gum that some girl wanted Joe to chew on! I could never figure that one out at all, but you've got to keep the fans happy, right? I didn't like the taste though. It wasn't really my brand.

A lot of young girls, of course, ask for a lock of Joe's hair. If we honored that request just half the time, not only would Joe not have long hair, he wouldn't have any hair. Just for kicks, though, I did send off a lock once, and Potey, Joe's dog, didn't seem to mind the snip at all.

Less than one percent of the letters are critical of Joe, but every time I read a piece of hate mail I wonder about these people who are trying to save him from the grip of Satan. I remember one letter in particular:

Dear Joe,

You are a real bum. Do you know that little children see you on television and that they copy you? Being a drunk, a tramp, and a draft dodger are things I could overlook. But your long hair has started a lot of little children taking drugs. I think you should get a haircut and clean up your act.

Sincerely,

People who write things like that have my sympathy. It's just so obvious they don't know Joe at all and probably wouldn't take the time even if they had the chance.

The funniest letters of all are the ones that accuse Joe of being some kind of oversexed Warren Beatty. I must admit I was a little startled a few years ago when I saw this huge mirror above the bed in Joe's New York apartment. To tell the truth, it scared the hell out of me; back home we would have looked up at cracked plaster. Joe smiled kind of slyly and said, "It's just something different, I guess."

When President Nixon's famous "Enemies" list was revealed in 1973 during the Senate Watergate hearings, I was amazed to find Joe's name right up there with certain congressmen, radicals, and other alleged foes of the Republic. But Joe had a simple explanation. "You see, Mom," he said, "Henry Kissinger was a bachelor then and they say he really liked his women. I guess the White House considered me too much competition for good ole Henry to handle."

Joe was kidding, of course (at least I think he was), but if he didn't go out with girls and take a drink now and then and even raise a little Cain from time to time, I'd think something was wrong. Joe isn't perfect. Even in Beaver Falls he can be rude and argumentative sometimes when he flies into town after a long business trip. Who doesn't have a bad day every now and then?

And as far as his long hair goes, even I sometimes think he lets it get a little too shaggy. When that happens, I just call him up and threaten to fly to wherever he is and cut it myself if he doesn't run to a barbershop. I did it once, too.

I can't complain at all about the fan mail, though, the good and the bad. I've answered over 32,000 letters myself over the years, and I've loved every second of it. The people who write them are his fans, and they are the ones who make everything possible for him. I love the letters from the kids, from the adults, even from the nuts—and I'd go so far as to accept a letter from Pete Rozelle, should he ever care to drop a line. Joe's fans are his success, and he realizes this more than anybody. When those cards and letters stop coming in, I'll know that Joe Namath is on the road to the world of the forgotten heroes.

But that's not going to happen for a while yet, if the good Lord sees fit to keep Joe's body together for a few more years.

TEN

I've already talked about some of Joe's injuries through the years, but right now I'd like to explain his medical history in full detail so that maybe you'll get the idea that the life of a professional football player isn't always a bed of roses. There's no better place to begin than with his knees.

As I mentioned earlier, Joe's knee problems might have stemmed from that time in his childhood when he had a terrible fever and his legs hurt so badly he could hardly stand it. But I don't think so, because the first time anything serious happened was in Joe's senior year of college during the Alabama-North Carolina State game. Two weeks later against Florida, Joe's right knee collapsed again in the very same way—he sprinted out to the right and just fell down without anybody touching him. This time, however, when the doctors drained his knee, the fluid contained blood, and right away Joe knew something was seriously wrong. When he reinjured it a third time during practice a few days before the Orange Bowl game against Texas, it just confirmed what he already knew.

That first operation in January of 1965 was performed by Dr. James Nicholas, who handles all the Jets and, it seems, most of the other athletes in the New York area as well. When Dr.

Nicholas made a three-inch incision on the inside of Joe's knee behind the kneecap, he discovered part of the cartilage had separated from the bone and had actually doubled over on itself. Not only did this cause pain, but it also meant Joe couldn't fully extend his leg. It was kind of like what happens when you jam a piece of wood in the crack of a door: the hinge in Joe's knee simply wouldn't work. So Dr. Nicholas cut it out. Cartilage acts only as a cushion for the knee and doesn't affect the knee's ability to work. It's like removing the shock absorbers from a car. You can go just as fast, but the ride's going to be bumpier.

Dr. Nicholas also tightened and pleated a couple of loose tendons, did some exploratory cutting on the right, or lateral, side of the knee which revealed nothing wrong, and as a bonus removed a small cyst from beneath the kneecap itself.

The rehabilitation began immediately, as I've already noted. When Joe woke up in the recovery room, Dr. Nicholas was grabbing on to Joe's right ankle and telling him to lift his leg. For three or four weeks he had to extend that hurt leg 50 times a day and "twitch" it—tighten it up with dynamic tension—400 times a day. Apparently if you don't start those exercises right away, the knee will atrophy so much it will never again regain its full strength.

"There's a sign in the Alabama locker room that says pain is all in the mind," Joe told a reporter at the time. "Maybe that's true, but I think I'll call Coach Bryant and tell him it hurts in the knee all the same."

Then began a game of musical knees. Joe tended to favor his hurt knee, the right one, with the unfortunate result that bursitis developed in the left knee. When the bursitis got troublesome enough, Joe started to favor his left knee, which put an undue strain back on the right—a condition which was not alleviated at all when the knee got clobbered after the whistle in an exhibition game against the Houston Oilers in 1966. Joe played the full season, but right afterwards Dr. Nicholas went to work on that poor right knee again, shifting around some more tendons in an effort to build up its strength.

Everything seemed to be okay. In 1967 Joe became the first quarterback in the history of professional football to throw for more than 4,000 yards. But in March of 1968 Dr. Nicholas got out his tool kit again, this time to repair some damaged tendons in the left knee. Of course, everybody knows what happened that season: the Jets won the championship of the AFL's Eastern Division, the league title over Oakland, and the Super Bowl.

In between operations were assorted bumps and bruises, the worst being that shot Ben Davidson leveled at Joe late in the 1967 season which broke his right cheekbone. Joe just shrugged it off, though, and completed two touchdown passes after the injury; the following week he came back to complete eighteen of twenty-six passes for four touchdowns as the Jets walloped San Diego, 42–31.

But after the Super Bowl triumph there was more to come, medically speaking. In 1970 Joe broke his right wrist in a game against the Colts and was forced to miss the last nine games of the season. In 1971, during an exhibition game against the Detroit Lions, a fumble in the Jets backfield was recovered by Detroit's powerful linebacker Mike Lucci, who proceeded to run with it toward the Jets' goal. The only Jet player standing between Mike and a Lion touchdown was Joe. Although quarterbacks aren't encouraged to try such heroics, especially during the exhibition season, Joe tried to tackle him. The force of the collision with Lucci and another Lion, Paul Naumoff, again collapsed his right knee and forced a fourth knee operation. He missed the first ten regular-season games.

It's amazing how people can still wonder why Joe doesn't like exhibition games, or, as the National Football League front office prefers to call them, "preseason" games.

Then in 1973 Joe suffered a separated shoulder in the second game of the season and was out seven more games.

No wonder the Jets haven't won another Super Bowl since the 1968 season and only one more divisional championship, in 1969. There hasn't often been a Joe Namath around to lead them, and with him out of the lineup the team just isn't the same.

Joe's importance to the Jets can be summed up in two words: intelligence and confidence. Professional football used to be a game of brute force, but the modern game combines strength with finesse. It's almost like a chess game the way a quarterback has to think several plays ahead and be able to pick out the tiniest flaw in the opponent's defense that, when exploited, will allow his team to attack successfully.

Confidence is a little harder to explain, but when Joe is in the game, everybody on the Jets seems to stand a little taller and play a little better. Eddie Bell, the Jets' wide receiver, put it this way:

"With Joe in there, without realizing it I think everybody just tries a little bit harder. We all know what Joe can do. If he checks off at the line of scrimmage, for example, we don't think about it at all. We know he's seen something, that he's called the supreme play. With another quarterback we might not feel quite the same way. When Joe calls a play, we have confidence it will work.

"I can't tell you the respect his teammates have for Joe. I look up to him as the finest quarterback of our era, if not in the history of the game. And the people he plays against feel that way, too. I'll never forget in 1971, the year Joe got hurt tackling Mike Lucci and couldn't play until the year was almost over. We were playing San Francisco in late November and Joe wasn't supposed to play even then, but Bob Davis, one of the backups, got hurt midway through the game and suddenly we didn't have *any* quarterbacks—except Joe. They were all injured, and we were behind, 14–0.

"Well, Joe came in and 65,000 people gave him a standing ovation. I looked over to the other bench and the San Francisco players were also applauding him. Now how many times do you see a football team applaud a guy who's trying to catch up and beat you? I could feel the chills running down my back. San Francisco respected Joe. They knew that when you play New York, you're playing Joe Namath. It's not the same playing the Jets unless Joe Namath is in the game.

"And on the second or third pass he threw, he hit me in the corner of the end zone for a touchdown."

Besides Joe's frequent absences from the lineup, a number of injuries hindered or sidelined several Jets and eventually forced their retirement in the years immediately following their Super Bowl triumph. The most notable retiree was Matt Snell, the big fullback who had been so important to the Jets during their drive to the title and then in the Super Bowl itself. Other key players like Don Maynard and George Sauer also left the Jets.

It's an unfortunate fact of life, especially if you're a Jets fan, that it takes time to rebuild a team that suddenly loses the services of a lot of veterans. Even Weeb Ewbank, their brilliant coach, decided to retire following the 1973 season in favor of his son-in-law, Charlie Winner. Joe would be the first to admit that no one player, no matter how good he is or what position he plays, can win a championship all by himself. Football is a team sport, from the star quarterback and the coaching staff right down to the last man on the taxi squad.

With so many teams in the league—twenty-six—it's hard to replace a lot of lost talent through the annual draft of college players. If you're the best team in the league, you only get the twenty-sixth pick on each round. Even if you draft well, it takes three or four years for those young collegians to develop fully as professionals, just as it did with Joe. The result has been a new order in the NFL, with former powerhouses such as the Jets and the Colts giving way to clubs like the Miami Dolphins and the Pittsburgh Steelers, which a few years ago were among the worst teams in the business.

Despite injuries and the general decline of the Jets, however, there have been a lot of great afternoons for Joe since the Super Bowl.

Two of the greatest came at opposite ends of the 1972 season. On September 24 in Baltimore, the second week of the year, Joe and Johnny Unitas just went crazy throwing the football, absolutely crazy. Joe would throw a touchdown pass and Johnny would throw a touchdown pass and then they'd let their field goal kickers have some fun and then they'd go back and throw some more touchdown passes: Namath to Bell, sixty-seven yards for a touchdown; Unitas to Havrilak, forty yards for a touchdown; Namath to Riggins, sixty-seven yards for a touchdown; Namath to Maynard, twenty-one yards; Namath to Caster, ten yards; Namath to Caster, seventy-nine yards; Unitas to Matte, twenty-one yards; Namath to Caster, eighty yards. When the carnage was over, Joe had thrown twenty-eight passes and completed fifteen for 496 yards—the third highest total in the history of pro football—and six touchdowns, while Unitas had completed twenty-six of forty-five for 376 yards and two touchdowns. Not incidentally, the Jets won, 44–34.

An even greater performance came against Oakland on December 12. Almost all of the Jets' running backs were hurt, and early in the game both of Joe's ankles were rapped so severely he couldn't run either. There was nothing he could do except take those three or four steps back and throw the ball, which he did forty-eight times. Twenty-five passes were completed against a defense that knew he was going to throw the ball on every play, and although the Jets lost, 24–16, it may have been the finest single-game performance of his career. And it was done right there on Monday Night Football in front of Howard Cosell, Dandy Don Meredith, and everybody else in the entire world.

And early in the 1974 season, Joe had another tremendous Monday night against the Miami Dolphins, the defending Super Bowl champions. In the first half, Miami dominated play completely and walked off the field with a 14–0 lead. But in the second thirty minutes Joe and the Jets made a ball game out of it. Joe engineered a careful, intelligent seventy-two-yard touchdown drive by passing seven times to John Riggins, the last of them for a nine-yard touchdown. A Jets' field goal made it 14–10 at the end of three. Miami scored a touchdown to go ahead 21–10, but Joe then hooked up with Rich Caster to complete the longest pass in Jets' history, eighty-nine yards, for a touchdown that closed the gap to 21–17. And in the final minutes, Joe kept plugging and plugging at the tough Miami defense until Miami's Jake Scott intercepted a pass with just thirteen seconds left. Joe would say it was a bad game because the Jets lost, but anybody who watched would have to disagree.

Indeed, although the Jets won only one of their first eight games last year, they showed signs of resurgence in the second half of the season by finishing up with six straight victories, including wins over two of the teams that made the play-offs, Buffalo and those same Dolphins.

So, after a few down years—the kind that happen to any team in any sport—it looks like the Jets might be right back in the thick of things in 1975. I've been told by Joe to expect another Super Bowl victory for the tenants of Shea Stadium before very long.

But what about Joe himself? In 1973 Joe's third long-term contract with the Jets expired, and he didn't sign a new one. Instead, he chose to play out his option and on May 1, 1975, became free to negotiate with any NFL club he wanted to.

Right away that journalistic rumor mill switched into high gear again. There were all sorts of wild stories that Joe was finally going to quit football forever, or become a part-owner of the Jets, or jump to the Canadian Football League, or become a television broadcaster, or sign with the Chicago Wind—now there's a name—of the new World Football League. As usual, it appeared to me that most of the press did its writing without checking with the best source of all—Joe Namath.

Well, as the song says, "When you're a Jet, you're a Jet all the way/ From your first cigarette to your last dying day," and even as this is being written I've heard from a *very* reliable source that Joe Namath has made up his mind and will be in a Jets uniform when the 1975 season opens. He's definitely going to be a part of the action when the next Super Bowl pennant is won by those guys in the Kelly green and white.

So that takes care of Joe's immediate future. He's only thirty-two years old and considering the life expectancy of a top quarterback—which is considerably longer than that of a running back, for example, or a guard—he should have several good seasons left. That's assuming, of course, his poor knees just don't give up the fight, which is always a possibility. Football is the most important thing in the world to Joe right now and I love watching him perform, but I would never want him to continue playing if there was any chance at all that he could permanently injure his legs. And he won't.

When his playing days are over, what then? It's a question a lot of people ask me, but I just can't answer it. The last time I really helped Joe make an important decision was when he went to the University of Alabama, and I'm not even sure how much I had to do with that choice. These days I read about Joe in the newspaper just like everybody else—then I call Joe and find out the facts.

One thing for sure. Joe is set financially even if he never plays another game of football in his life. Right from the beginning Joe has had good people around to help him take care of his money, especially Jimmy Walsh, and he's invested wisely through a series of corporations set up in his name. He owns several restaurants around the country and apartments in Fort Lauderdale, Birmingham, and Tuscaloosa, so he'll always have a roof over his head. Oh, a couple of things haven't worked out, like the Broadway Joe's fast-food franchise and the Namath Girls and Mantle Boys temporary employment agency (I've often wondered how Mantle—that's Mickey Mantle, natural-ly—got stuck with the boys while Joe got the girls), but he's got a pretty solid completion average in the business department.

And of course there are always the endorsements, including everything from chairs to popcorn machines to football games for armchair quarterbacks. After all these years I must admit I still get a charge out of seeing Joe on television, even when he does something pretty strange like that pantyhose commercial he made a few years ago. Goodness! But in January of 1975 he signed a very good contract with the nice people over at Arrow Shirts, so I guess things even out.

When Joe does retire, though, I'm sure he won't be content to just sit back and relax. He's got too much energy for that, and I'm also sure that whatever he chooses to do, he'll be just as big a success as he has been on the football field. No question about it.

There are a couple of things about Joe's future that bother me sometimes, and I guess like most mothers I tend to nag Joey about them. The first is his college degree, or rather his lack of it. In all the excitement and activity that followed the 1965 Orange Bowl game, Joe never did finish out his senior year at Alabama and right now he's fifteen credits short of his bachelor of arts degree. I know it's tough for somebody to go back to college after he's been away for ten or fifteen years, and I also understand that maybe a college degree isn't as valuable to have when you're thirty-five or so as it is when you're twenty-one or twenty-two. Still, nobody in my family has gotten a college degree. I suppose it's an old hang-up of mine that comes from the fact that I, myself, only had the opportunity to attend school through the twelfth grade, but I will be very happy and very proud the day Joe walks through that front door with a sheepskin instead of a pigskin in his hand.

Joe has promised me he's going to get that degree, too, and he has often mentioned not only that he'd like to come back to Beaver Falls to live but that he'd like to teach here as well. I can't think of anybody who could do a better job working with kids than my Joey.

The other thing I'd really like is for Joe to get married—and I understand there are one or two young ladies out there who might like the idea, too. His brothers and sister have already done their part in giving me my eighteen grandchildren and one great-grandchild, and I think it's about time for Joe to start doing his share. I know he can't stay single forever, but I'll be darned if he isn't doing a good job so far. Who knows? Maybe one of these days it'll happen.

So that's just about it: a mother's story about her famous son. To most people, I guess, Joe Namath will always be the "Broadway Joe" of football fame, but that part of his life is just a small portion of the Joe Namath story, the tip of the iceberg. If this book has allowed you to learn more about his life and understand what Joe is really like, it will have achieved its purpose.

Last Christmas, Joe came home for the holidays. There was no parade, no celebration, and no banquet. Just Joe and his brothers, their families, and their friends. I served up some liver and dumpling soup, an old Hungarian favorite, and I couldn't help but think about how life had changed for all of us.

If somebody had told me fifteen or twenty years ago we would all be living the kind of life we live today, I never would have believed him. It seems as though it's all been a dream. Actually two dreams: first, a nightmare of struggle and near-poverty; second, a fantasy of success and prosperity. But I would never change a minute of my life even if I could. Having had to struggle during those early years made the good times, when they finally came, all that much better. And I know Joe feels the same way. I remember my first dinner with Joe in New York right after he'd signed with the Jets. He gave the waitress a $20 tip and I just about fell off my chair. Then I chuckled to myself as I remembered that long-ago day when Joe's father came home with a paycheck for exactly ten cents.

Maybe it's the little mind-jogging experiences like that which allow me to enjoy every minute of every day. And as far as tomorrow goes, well, tomorrow is going to be even better.

And so, to all the Joe Namath fans of the world, I pray your blessings will be a thousandfold. To all of you who aren't Joe Namath fans, may your blessings also be a thousandfold.